PROUDLY SUPPORTING Royal Air Force Benevolent Fund

63 AIRCRAFT TYPES FLOWN
IN WARTIME AND IN PEACE

IF IT HAD WINGS

THE UNIQUE AVIATION CAREER OF
SQN LDR. ERIC MARKWELL

ERIC MARKWELL
WITH ALAN MARKWELL

IFITHADWINGS.COM

This book is a memoir, based on a mix of recollection and historical fact. The authors have tried to recreate events, locales and conversations from their memories.

ISBN: 978-1-7394914-0-6

Published by Alan Markwell.

Editor: Claire Sanders / clairesanders.uk

Cover design, illustration, maps and interior formatting:
Mark Thomas / Coverness.com

DEDICATION

This book is dedicated to Squadron Leader Eric Markwell, whose story it tells.

Eric trained in Canada as part of the British Commonwealth Air Training Plan. He was one of around 137,000 others, many of whom did not survive the war. It seems appropriate therefore to also dedicate this book to those who trained in Canada and other locations around what was then the British Empire and who, in many cases, paid the ultimate price for the freedom that we enjoy today.

British Commonwealth Air Training Plan Memorial
Elvington, Yorkshire

The authors, Alan (left) and Eric (right), sharing their love of aviation in the Shuttleworth Collection Bristol Fighter, on 11th July 1988.

FOREWORD

My late father Eric Markwell came from a simple country background (his father was a jobbing gardener) and in common with so many others found himself caught up in the Second World War.

Equally in common with so many of his generation, Eric was very modest about his life achievements and didn't tell stories of the war. I'd often asked him to write down his experiences, which he was seemingly reluctant to do, but in his final years he wrote this manuscript with a view to leaving it with his family on the understanding that it should not be published until after he had died.

However, when Eric did pass away, there was still a portion of his story left to tell.

In order that the reader can learn about the full breadth of his career, this book is split into two main Parts.

Part 1 is written mostly by Eric - with some additional narrative from myself - and details his life from 1938-1961.

In Part 2, I tell the remainder of my father's story.

Taken together, I hope that this book serves as a testament to Eric's achievements and the incredible life that he led. I very much hope you enjoy reading his unique story.

ALAN MARKWELL

JULY 2023

PROUDLY SUPPORTING Royal Air Force Benevolent Fund

ABOUT THE ROYAL AIR FORCE BENEVOLENT FUND

Against the background of writing '*If It Had Wings*', both of the authors felt it important to highlight the work of the Royal Air Force Benevolent Fund.

The Royal Air Force Benevolent Fund is the Royal Air Force's leading welfare charity, providing financial, practical and emotional support to serving and former members of the RAF – regardless of rank – as well as their partners and dependents.

The Fund helps members of the RAF Family deal with a wide range of issues: from childcare and relationship difficulties to injury and disability, and from financial hardship and debt to illness and bereavement. Any member of the RAF Family can approach the Fund for help, including serving and former members of the RAF, their partners and dependents.

A portion of the proceeds from this book will be donated to the Fund.

To find out more about the organisation's work – including how to get involved and how to donate – please visit:

rafbf.org

TABLE OF CONTENTS

The earliest known photo of Eric Markwell, seen here with his father - Henry Markwell - and his father's cousin, Pollie.

PROLOGUE

FAMILY BACKGROUND

My father, Eric Markwell was born on 17th August 1923 in Rotherham, South Yorkshire. At the time, his parents Henry and Elizabeth (apparently known to everyone as Lizzie), lived at Low Grange Farm in Thurnscoe. It's not clear what role my grandfather filled on the farm but it's reasonable to assume that he was a farm labourer. Henry had been born in 1886 in Ely (Cambridgeshire) and served in both the Gloucestershire and Royal Warwickshire regiments during the First World War. We know that he served in Egypt as we had a photo of him seated on a camel in front of the pyramids (sadly the photograph was lost after he died). How he ended up in Yorkshire is not known but he had met Lizzie and they married in December 1918.

Low Grange Farmhouse is still there although surrounded by a large estate. It's Grade 2 listed which no doubt saved it from the demolition that took place to all the outbuildings. Following my family's return from Singapore in 1968, we visited dad's cousin Pollie who still lived at Low Grange Farm in the 1970s. By this time, the farmhouse was quite run down although it has been greatly smartened up since then.

Henry and Lizzie must have moved shortly after Eric was born. I have a single reference to moving from Bristol in 1928 so there is a gap in our family knowledge between 1923 and 1928. On the assumption that there was no intermediate move, the family moved to Park Hatch Estate near Godalming in Surrey in or around 1928 where Henry had taken the position of Head Gardener and where Eric grew up. The reader will note Eric's references to living in the countryside on large estates. In those days, Park Hatch was a Palladian mansion with extensive grounds and gardens owned by the Godman family. It was demolished after the Second World War but has been replaced by a smaller house and the grounds restored by new owners.

Eric left Godalming Grammar School in August 1940 having passed eight subjects at what was then the General Certificate of Education. Whilst at GGS he met twin sisters, Muriel (whom everyone called Georgie) and Vivien Templemore who, though he did not know it, were to play an important part in his life. Later that year Eric joined Barclays Bank in Haslemere where it turned out that Vivien also worked. Eric stayed with the bank until he applied for enlistment in March 1942.

Eric with his parents (left and centre) and two unknown relatives.

Twins Muriel (left) and Vivien

Eric in his ARP (Air Raid Precautions) uniform,1939.

PART 1
1938 - 1961

PRE-WAR, WARTIME AND POST-WAR

ERIC MARKWELL
(WITH ALAN MARKWELL)

UNITED KINGDOM

SEPT 1942 - JUNE 1943

SEPT 1942 - JUNE 1943

1. ABERYSTWYTH *

2. HEATON PARK, MANCHESTER

3. ANTSY*, COVENTRY

* STATIONS AT WHICH ERIC SERVED

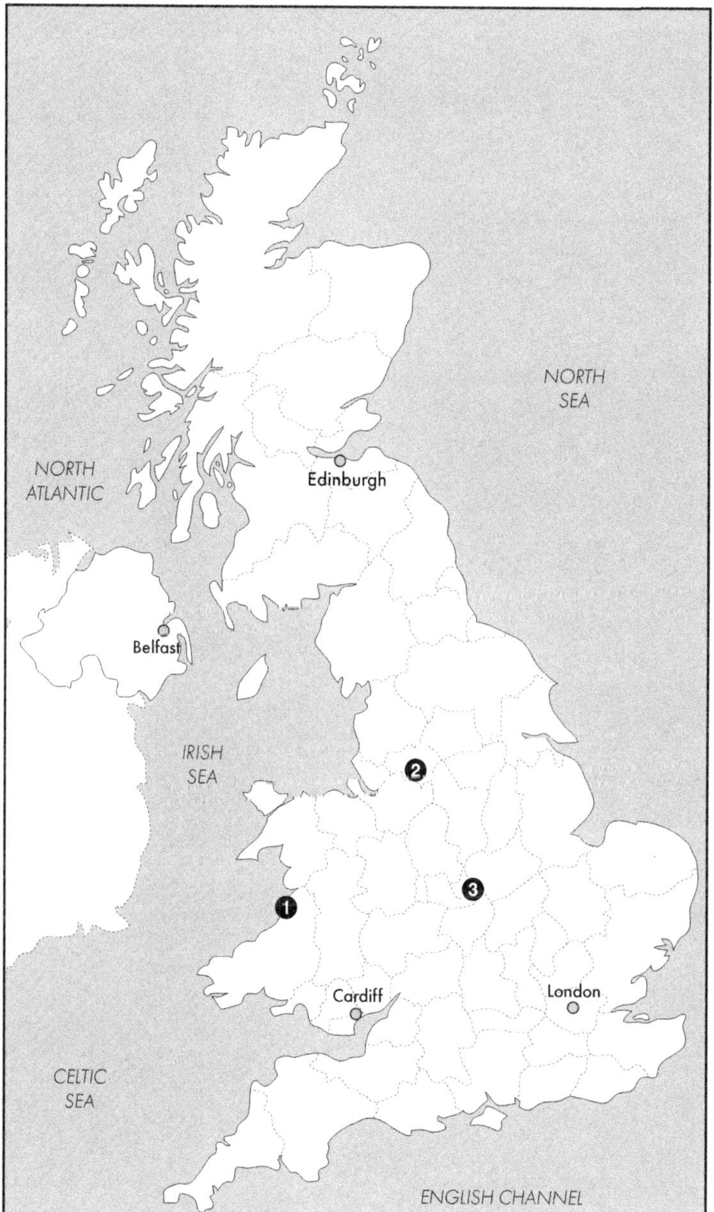
NORTH SEA
NORTH ATLANTIC
Edinburgh
Belfast
IRISH SEA
2
3
1
Cardiff
London
CELTIC SEA
ENGLISH CHANNEL

CHAPTER 1

HOW IT STARTED

It is difficult to know when I first became interested in aeroplanes and aviation. My childhood was spent living fairly deep in the countryside on large estates, where my father was Head Gardener – aeroplanes were virtually unheard of. I have a vague memory of a visit to a nearby town in (I think) 1935 to see Sir Alan Cobham's Flying Circus. My next contact with aeroplanes came in two visits to Navy Days when I saw Fleet Air Arm biplanes (Hawker Nimrods) simulating bombing attacks on ships and a visit to HMS Courageous, the aircraft carrier. My main interest in 1938 was ships, particularly battleships and at that time I did consider a career in the Royal Navy when I eventually left school.

During 1938, as a result of the horrors of bombing seen in the Spanish Civil War and with the prospect of war with Germany looming, the Air Raid Precautions (ARP) was formed to protect the civil population in the event of air attack. The aeroplane was front-page news.

I joined the ARP as a messenger and when war eventually came, in my last year at school, I was made a Warden and trained in anti-gas precautions, first aid and rescue.

Then in 1940 came the Battle of Britain. Living in Surrey, as we were, much of it was fought overhead and like so many of my generation, aeroplanes became our main object of interest. In 1941 that interest was given shape by the formation of the Air Training Corps (ATC).

I had left school in the autumn of 1940 and was working in a local bank, but my old school had formed its own squadron (No. 664) and I was able to join, becoming its first Non-Commissioned Officer (NCO). The training received (foot drill, aeroplane recognition, navigation, a little theory of flight and Morse code) stood me in good stead later. The squadron was affiliated to RAF Farnborough and in the summer, we spent a day sampling RAF life, which included a flight in an Anson aeroplane. I was determined from then that flying was my aim.

CHAPTER 2

ENLISTMENT

On 24th March 1942, I donned my ATC uniform with my recently acquired Sergeant's stripes, presented myself at the nearest RAF recruiting office in Reading and volunteered for aircrew training. A couple of short written tests plus an interview later and it was off to Reading Station clutching a railway warrant bound for Oxford. Once at Oxford Station, the Railway Transport Officer (RTO) directed me to one of the university buildings, which was the RAF Recruitment Centre. Then followed a further written test, an interview by a board of officers and an aptitude test.

For this test, we sat in a simulated aeroplane cockpit with a wooden control column and a simulated throttle lever on the left side. In front of the victim was a screen (we would now call it a cathode ray tube (CRT)) on which a spot of light moved in an erratic manner. Below the screen was a series of three red lights which flashed on and off at irregular intervals. The test was to try and move the spot of light to the centre of the screen, hold it there and simultaneously, as a red light came on, extinguish it by forward movement of the throttle before the light went out.

We were given two runs on the machine; the first a practice, the second the real test. No result was given. Then came the real crunch - the aircrew medical, again no result was given.

We were then sent to a waiting room before being called for another interview, at which the results of all the tests were given. To my delight, I had passed. I was however warned that I would be enrolled in the Pilot, Navigator, Air Bomber (PNB) Scheme where my eventual aircrew trade would be decided on the results that I achieved in my future training, although I had expressed a preference for pilot (most volunteers did).

Having accepted this ruling, I joined a group of other successful applicants and together we swore an oath of allegiance to King George VI and became members of the Royal Air Force Volunteer Reserve (RAFVR).

Anti-climax followed; we were given a small RAFVR lapel badge and sent home to await call-up, forecast a month or two away - we were on 'deferred service'.

A frustrating period of waiting followed. In August came my nineteenth birthday and still no call-up - until the beginning of September. As I came home from the office, my mother's face said it all. The envelope from the Air Ministry had arrived. I was to report to the Aircrew Reception Centre (ACRC) at

Lord's Cricket Ground[1] in London on 29th September 1942. Enclosed were full instructions plus the inevitable (one way) railway warrant.

Eric, in ATC uniform with Sergeant's stripes.

1 See *Historical Context* section, page 213, for more informaton.

CHAPTER 3

AIRCREW RECEPTION CENTRE (ACRC)

Following the instructions given, I duly presented myself at Lord's on 29th September. I was directed to one of the entrances to the pavilion where, once inside, RAF administration took over. As it often does in such circumstances, it progressed me smoothly forward and in less than one hour I had been fully documented. I was now Aircraftman 2nd Class (A/C 2) Markwell E. No. 1604625, Trade Aircraft Hand/General Duties (ACH/GD) and the lowest form of life known to the RAF. The rate of pay was two shillings, sixpence (twelve and a half pence) per day.

With administration over, it was yet another medical, called the Free from Infection (FFI), details of which are better glossed over.

We then went outside to be formed into Flights and marched from Lord's towards Regent's Park and a large block of flats taken over for the duration by the RAF. The basement of this block had been turned into a large Airmen's Mess where we would take all our meals for the rest of our stay at ACRC.

Having as yet no 'irons' (knife, fork, spoon) of our own, we were issued with one spoon each to be used for both courses of the meal. I don't remember what we ate but the spoon was adequate. As we left the Mess we were introduced to a large tub of boiling water with a scum of grease on top in which we were to wash our irons. This was to be a feature of all our future Messes.

Mustered once more into our Flights by our Corporal, it was off to another block of flats where we were introduced to the 'Airman's Refuge' - his bed space. Each bed space contained an iron bed plus a small bedside locker. On the bed were three blankets and three 'biscuits' (a mattress split into three components).

The whole area of the bed space measured approximately four feet by six feet, and it was all ours. It was surprising how many beds could fit into each room. I was lucky; I got the space near the (small) bathroom where I had an extra six inches between my bed and the wall opposite the bath, against which my bed was jammed.

Having had a chance to see our 'home' for the next three weeks, we were called down to receive a pep talk from the officer who would be our Commanding Officer (CO). He turned out to have been a cashier in one of the other banks in the town where I had worked and I knew him - small world. He acknowledged me but that was all. Our relationship was always formal and I neither received any favours nor did I expect them.

From the CO and our Corporal, we were given an outline of what we would be doing, and the few basic rules that would apply to us. In particular, 'Wakey Wakey', 'Lights Out' and the need to book out at the Guardroom if we left the building surrounds, unless accompanied by an NCO. With all this hopefully digested, it was back down to the Airmen's Mess (spoon in hand) for supper then back to our 'home', now designated our 'billet'.

The rest of the evening was free to get to know our immediate neighbours and make up our beds (no sheets) before 'Lights Out'. I found that our Entry included several ex-Metropolitan Policemen; RAF aircrew was the only branch of any of the services they could join as they were classed as being in a 'reserved occupation' and so not subject to compulsory military service. They were very good company and obviously knew London well, which was a bonus for those of us who were strangers to the capital.

The next day saw the beginning of the conversion of what our Corporal called 'a bunch of scruffy civilians', into airmen. It began with breakfast (spoons again for the last time) and then off to 'Stores' for the issue of uniforms and other equipment. Much fun was made on the radio at the time of this aspect of service life. In reality it was an efficient operation.

At the beginning of a long counter, we were given a kitbag and as we moved along the line, we collected two uniforms comprising: two shirts with four collars, a greatcoat, a cap with white 'flash' (Trainee Aircrew), two pairs of boots, a tie, underwear, socks, towels, webbing equipment, a respirator, an anti-gas cape, a steel helmet, a set of irons, a button-stick and finally a 'Housewife' (small sewing kit) for small clothing repairs. Heavily laden, it was back to our billet to change into uniform and visit the tailor where any badly fitting items were marked for alteration. Surprisingly, there were not many.

The rest of the day was taken up with marking each item of kit with our serial number and being marched down to the Mess for meals, to use our new irons and of course try and clean them in the dreaded greasy tub. As far as I know, no one caught anything from this method of cleaning one's cutlery, but it was used extensively on many RAF Stations.

Being now fully kitted out, our formal training started. Foot drill and Physical Training (PT) were constant themes. It was during foot drill that I had my first contact with RAF 'Sick Parade'. After a couple of days of drill and marching my feet became very painful, so I reported sick.

This involved packing a small haversack with toilet gear and reporting to our Corporal before morning parade, to be marched to Sick Quarters (the Medical Centre) some distance away in Regent's Park. Asked by the Corporal what was the problem, I said 'my feet hurt'. I was told to march up and down (hobble really), to be diagnosed.

The diagnosis was: 'Your boots are too small, up to Stores and change them'. The fault was my own. Ordinarily, I wore a size seven and a half; I found that the RAF did not do half sizes so had asked for a size seven when I should have had an eight. Once issued with the eights I had no further foot troubles. I got a very large 'rocket' from the Flight Sergeant at Stores for my sins.

Interspersed with sessions of drill and PT, we were lectured on various aspects of Service life and RAF law. There was also a series of lectures from the Medical Officer (MO) about aspects of living in a close contact community and on contact with the opposite sex. Lectures were given to the whole of our Entry (some 600 people) in the Odeon cinema at Swiss Cottage. It was at that time that I learned what led to the 'Old Sweats' dictum of 'never volunteer for nothing'.

We were paraded after lunch one day and the CO asked if any of us had been given any anti-gas training. Ignoring (or not seeing) the Corporal, behind the CO, shaking his head vigorously, some of us, myself included, said we had. As a result, we scrubbed the Guardroom floor whilst the others sat in the comfort of the cinema listening to an anti-gas lecture.

During the next week, we were marched down to the RAF Medical Centre at Abbey Lodge in Regent's Park for our inoculations (jabs). In the 1940s the jabs were given individually, not as a cocktail, as we are used to in modern medicine, also the needles were re-used for anything up to fifty times. It could be quite a painful procedure. Our first jab was Typhoid and Paratyphoid (TAB) and having received it, we were marched back to our billet where we were surprised to be given the rest of the day off. We soon found out why, as within a few hours we were all shivering and with high temperatures; most of us ended up in bed wrapped in our blankets, with no further interest in the evening meal or any other activity.

The next morning, we all had very sore and stiff arms, to which our NCO reacted 'swing those arms' as he marched us around; there was no sympathy there. We subsequently had another TAB and also an Anti-tetanus (ATT) jab; these produced considerably less after-effects.

As part of our PT we were taken to the Seymour Hall Swimming Baths for a swimming test. As I could not then swim my documents were duly annotated 'non-swimmer'. This turned out to be a bonus at a later stage of training.

Not all of our time at ACRC was taken up with duty and training. There were some free evenings when we could go out to the Navy, Army and Air Force Institute (NAAFI), which served drinks and snacks, or if you knew London, as did our ex-Met policemen, you could find other places of entertainment. Wartime London was a dreary place after all the bombing and everywhere closed early in case the air raid sirens sounded, although at that time this did not happen often.

Our weekends were free and on the first, those of us who lived within a day return of London were given permission, if we wished, to take our civilian clothes home, on the condition that we must be back by 2200. I took advantage of this and surprised my parents by turning up on the doorstep in uniform for the first time to spend an hour or two with them before returning to ACRC. On the second weekend, I went with two of the ex-policemen to Stamford Bridge to watch Chelsea play football.

By the third week in London we were, in our Corporal's words 'beginning to look like airmen', and the question of our posting began to loom large. At the time, there was something of a logjam in the training system so instead of going on to Initial Training Wing (ITW) as was the plan, some previous entries had gone to an Aircrew Camp at Ludlow in Shropshire. Here, the Commander of the Flying Training Group had an estate on which the camp was established where the Under Training (U/T) aircrew were engaged in estate work on the site.

Reports coming back were not encouraging, so no one wanted to go there. Luckily when our postings came through, we found that we were posted to No. 6 ITW at Aberystwyth in Wales, the smallest and most remote of the ITWs.

The morning of 24th October found us in full webbing equipment comprising a large pack, a small pack, a water bottle, a respirator and a steel helmet, loading our kitbags on to an RAF truck and ourselves into two similar vehicles, bound for Euston and then on to Wales.

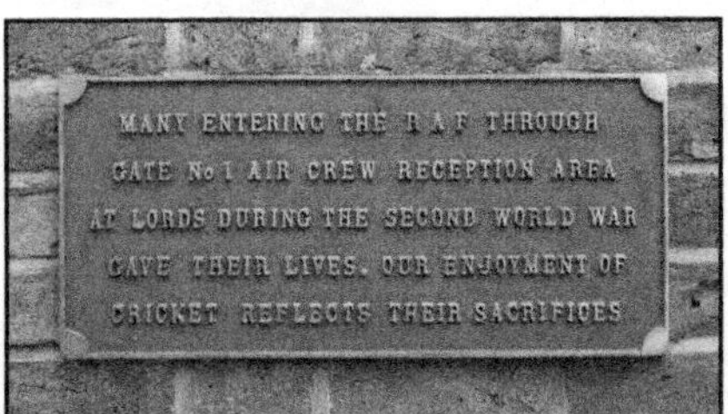

This plaque at Lord's commemorates those who passed through and ultimately gave their lives for the freedom we enjoy.

CHAPTER 4

PROFESSIONAL TRAINING

The training we had received in London had been of a nature common to most new recruits to the RAF. Our posting to ITW signified the beginning of our aircrew training, still however to the three aircrew trades (PNB), under which we had enlisted.

At the end of a tedious train journey from Euston, inevitably through Crewe Junction, we finally arrived at Aberystwyth Station, where a small reception committee of NCOs, headed by a Sergeant who was to become our Drill Instructor (DI) and Flight NCO met us. Kitbags were loaded into a truck and we, loaded by full kit, were marched off to our billet, a requisitioned hotel on the seafront. This short march proved to be our first surprise.

In London, we had been trained to march at the RAF standard speed of 120 paces per minute. Here we were told in no uncertain terms that we would now be marching at 140 paces per minute with a 27-inch pace rather than the standard

30-inch one. It came as something of a shock to be dashing along at Light Infantry/Gurkha speed.

At our billet, we were allocated our rooms (an average of five beds to a room) and here we received our second surprise. On our beds were the normal three 'biscuits', as well as a small bolster and two sheets – an absolute luxury. We were seeing the first small difference between U/T aircrew and other airmen.

Having gotten out of our webbing equipment and other appendages, it was down to the basement (which was our Mess), for a meal and a formal meeting with our DI. Having run through what he expected of us and given us our instructions for the next morning, we were sent back upstairs to unpack and to study the photograph behind the door, which showed us how we were to make-up our beds and to lay out our kit before work each day.

In essence the 'biscuits' were to be stacked at the head of the bed in front of the bolster, with two blankets and two sheets interleaved on top, wrapped in the third blanket. Our towel was then spread over the foot of the bed and on it, in a specific order: our toilet kit, our shoe and clothes brushes and our button stick. Below the bed stood our spare pair of boots, polished (soles too) backed by our small pack and water bottle. This was not too much of a problem, but what was not so easy, was to fold the anti-gas cape into an oblong squared-off shape and attach it to the wall behind the bed, where previous occupants of the room had put up a network of tintacks, on which was stretched black thread to hold the cape flat against the wall. The rest of the webbing equipment then had to be separated and laid out in a specific pattern. We had no lockers, so the rest of our kit was stowed in the kitbag under the bed.

The next morning it was Reveille at 0600 signalled by a loud shout from our DI downstairs. We then had thirty minutes to dress, shave and get downstairs for breakfast. With an average of five to a room, this required a fair amount of give and take from all.

From the start of breakfast on the first morning we were given an hour to get back to our rooms and lay out our kit. The rooms were then inspected by the DI who, as expected, went through everything very thoroughly. At the same time the Stores' NCO came around to issue us with white webbing belts that would replace the cloth uniform belt throughout our stay at ITW. Thus, it was easy to pick out the trainees from the permanent staff. The white belts had to be cleaned with white cleaner and the buckles, which were brass, had to be polished.

We were then called downstairs again and assembled in front of our billet for our first taste of drill, the ITW way. Before this however, we had to hand over our spare pair of boots, which were sent to the cobbler where the rubber soles were replaced by steel heel and toe plates and the soles hobnailed. It was intended that when we marched, we could hear ourselves and maintain the step. These were our drill boots and, needless to say, they had to be polished to a high gloss and maintained in that state and would be inspected by the eagle eye of the DI on every morning parade.

Next, it was on to foot drill, getting used to the 140 paces per minute.

For the next twenty weeks of our course at Aberystwyth our days followed a laid down pattern; morning drill parade, followed by lectures. The lectures covered: RAF law, navigation, theory of flight, meteorology, armaments (bombs and guns), Morse code (buzzer and lamp, to a standard of six words per minute on the lamp and eight words per minute on the buzzer), aeroplane recognition, engines and airframe theory, anti-gas training (including a run in the gas chamber, which proved the efficacy of the anti-gas respirator, as when at the end we had to remove it, our eyes promptly streamed with the effect of the tear gas), interspersed with the specialist 'trade' lectures.

The lectures were spread throughout the various parts of the university, so it meant quite a lot of marching between them and our billet. This, coupled with drill and PT parades with specialist Physical Training Instructors (PTIs), soon improved our physical fitness. Here, my non-swimmer status proved something of a bonus, as instead of doing PT on the seafront or running up and down the local hills, I, and several others were marched up to the university swimming baths and taught to swim. As the weather grew colder and greatcoats became the dress of the day this wasn't so good. The baths were up a very steep hill and at our marching speed we were arriving there sweating profusely. Representation was duly made to higher authority and we were allowed on swimming parade without greatcoats. To add to the fitness regime, Wednesday and Saturday afternoons were set aside for sport. For me, that meant swimming until I attained the required standard of two lengths of the pool thereafter I took up cross-country running.

Of the lectures, those on armaments were very detailed, concentrating on the Browning 303 machine gun, then the main armament of RAF fighters and bombers. At the end of the course we were required, as a final test, to completely strip and reassemble the gun blindfolded.

Armament training also included live range firing of the Browning, Lee Enfield 303 rifle and the .38 revolver - all enjoyable for a 'country boy', as I had shot with shotgun and .22 rifle from my early teens. We also had weekly visits to the clay pigeon range where we shot at twelve clays each visit. The armament officer had offered a prize of £1, for all twelve clays destroyed. No one had claimed it until I got lucky on our last visit and got the lot, plus £1. This was cause for celebration!

As our skill at foot drill increased, we were introduced to rifle drill and finally to the aircrew trainee speciality Continuity Drill. By the end of the course we could, as a Flight of some fifty men, carry out a sequence of drill in quick and slow time, covering all the foot and rifle drill movements in the drill book and extending over a time span of ten minutes with only the initial command of 'Marker' from the DI. Nowadays Continuity Drill is the speciality of the RAF Regiment Display Team who still use some of the tricks we were taught.

Coupled with all of the activity in the lecture room, the drill and PT sessions, came visits to the dentist where any doubtful teeth were filled. If any teeth contained a civilian filling, it was replaced by a specially insulated filling.

As we were at Aberystwyth for the whole of the winter, greatcoats were the order of the day, except for we non-swimmers going up the hill and drill parades. I have some vivid memories of standing on the seafront in bitter winds carrying out rifle drill, where my fingers were so cold that I could not feel the rifle and trying desperately not to commit the heinous crime of dropping it. I never did, but some of the others were unlucky and so ended up on a charge in front of the Squadron Commander.

Off-duty time was, to a great extent, taken up with study for the final exams, cleaning equipment and perhaps going to the small canteen for a snack and a soft drink (I did not drink alcohol during my training). There was a local cinema if one so wished and a weekly dance in the town hall. We usually went to these but otherwise there was little else to occupy our off-duty hours. Cutting into our time off there was also guard duty. If one was on guard it meant a night's duty on a 'four-on, four-off' routine which, depending on the shift you drew, left you feeling rather tired for duty the next day, which was a normal working day.

Coming in the middle of our course was Christmas 1942. In true RAF tradition, we were served our Christmas dinner by our officers and Senior Non-Commissioned Officers (SNCOs) and were given a couple of days off duty, then it was back to training.

Approaching the end of February 1943 came the final exams, further progress in aircrew training and re-grading (not promotion) to Leading Aircraftman (LAC) with a pay increase of sixpence (two and a half pence) per day, depending on the outcome of the exams. Luckily all went well, and I was duly told to put a 'Props' (Propellers, the badge of an LAC) on my uniforms. Next would come my first contact with flying – Grading School.

At that point I contracted jaundice that resulted in a week in Sick Quarters followed by ten days sick leave. The leave was welcome, the first since joining up, but it meant that I would miss my posting and those of the friends I had made.

The journey home was a reverse of our journey up to Aberystwyth and I arrived in London just in time to catch the last train to Guildford. From there, since the buses had stopped running hours before, I was faced with a nine-mile walk to my home. Despite the spell in Sick Quarters it was no problem, being helped halfway by a cup of tea in Godalming police station, having met a police patrol on my way through the town. I arrived home in the early hours of the morning and settled back into my own bed for the rest of the night.

At home I found some of my friends were also on leave from their various service units, so it was an opportunity to exchange news and to visit my old school and ATC Squadron to whom I gave a chat on what I had seen of the RAF so far.

Back at ITW, since my Flight had been replaced by the next

Entry, I was employed in Stores, awaiting the next Flight to be posted to Grading School.

On 14th April 1943 I left my 'home' of the last six months and, loaded down with kit, reported to the other squadron where I joined a Flight due to leave next day. I left with them for Grading School at Ansty, near Coventry, for my introduction to flying the Tiger Moth biplane. The course was to be of twelve hours flying, after which we would be assessed and our eventual aircrew trade determined.

Ansty gave us the standard RAF reception, documentation, billets, local rules etc. The difference here from our earlier postings was the living accommodation. Ansty was a permanent Station and the buildings were proper service design, so we had more space in our rooms.

First thing the next morning was a visit to Stores, to hand in one of our uniforms and receive in exchange, RAF Blue Battledress. No buttons to clean - joy! Battledress however was to be worn only for flying or duty; off the Station it was 'Best Blue'. We had left the white belts behind at ITW so now it was back to the standard belt. We then went on to be split up into Flights for flying. Some of the others and I would not do our flying at Ansty but at Southam. This entailed an aircrew coach journey of some length, night and morning, to get to Southam.

Loaded into the crew coach, we arrived at Southam the next morning to find that it was a grass field with some Nissen huts at one end. Once assembled and given the usual pep talk, it was off to draw flying kit, consisting of two sets of flying overalls (inner and outer), flying boots, gauntlets, a leather helmet and a parachute.

Following kitting-up we met our instructors. My instructor was the Deputy Flight Commander, a Pilot Officer (P/O). Flying was not on the agenda for the first day or two; it was back to the classroom for lectures covering the fuel and oil systems of the aeroplane and a demonstration on how to hand swing the propeller and not get hit.

Then followed live practice; that covered our first day of flying. We also discovered, to our joy, that as we were now flying, our pay would be increased by four shillings a day raising it to seven shillings, sixpence (thirty-seven and a half pence).

My logbook shows that on 18th April 1943 I had my first flight in Tiger Moth R 5012 with my instructor P/O Perkins. It followed what I came to know years later as 'Effects of Controls' with a look at the area around Southam.

A three-day break due to adverse weather conditions followed and then the real work started with a change of instructor to Sgt. Brown, with whom I flew the next three hours up to initial take-offs, circuits and landings (known as 'circuits and bumps'). A further change of instructor saw me trying to see beyond the head of Warrant Officer (W/O) Scott, who filled the front cockpit. The Eight-Hour Test came and was survived. After this it was concentration on circuits and bumps before the final Twelve-Hour Test. One or two of the students went solo in the latter stages of the course. I did not make it to solo and found the Tiger Moth something of a struggle, being, according to W/O Scott 'too heavy footed', so much so, that he made me wear plimsolls instead of flying boots. It was not a requirement of the course that we went solo, but it was a bonus for those who did as it pointed to a good chance that they would be recommended for pilot training.

On completion of flying (twelve hours, forty-five minutes) we had a few days to wait, for everyone to finish their hours. I found myself detailed for guard duty and patrolling the line of aeroplanes carrying a rifle (unloaded) at various times of the night. One memorable day, Geoffrey De Havilland did a 'beat-up' in a Mosquito that was just off the secret list - very exciting!

Postings duly came up and as expected we were all posted to the Aircrew Dispersal Centre (ACDC) at Heaton Park in Manchester. Before going there however there was a matter of fourteen days embarkation leave at home.

To reach my home at Dunsfold in Surrey involved a journey by train to London, a further train to Godalming and finally a bus to Dunsfold. Loaded down with full webbing equipment, plus a respirator and steel helmet, it was somewhat daunting. Luckily our kitbags with our flying clothing were sent to Heaton Park to await our arrival, but it was still a fair load.

In London, a friendly soldier from one of the Guards Regiments carried my large pack for me, but at Waterloo I found the train was only going as far as Guildford, so as on my earlier sick leave I was faced with a nine-mile walk, carrying full kit this time. Again, the police in Godalming helped out with a cup of tea. In wartime, everyone helped others where possible.

Once at home, my leave followed the pattern of the previous one. I went into Godalming to see if any of my friends were also on leave, visited my old school to catch up on news of other friends in the Services and visited the ATC Squadron where the CO asked if I would give them some instruction in Continuity Drill. They seemed to enjoy it and proved quite good at a few of the basic drill movements.

I also visited the bank in Haslemere where I had worked and was invited home to tea by one of the girls with whom I had worked. At her home, I found that her twin sister, who worked at another branch of the bank, was also home. I had known the twins at school, where in my last year they had joined the school on evacuation from London. After tea, the sister kept me company on the walk to the railway station. Neither of us at that time had any idea that some five years later we would walk down the aisle of a local church together, at the end of our marriage service.

In the final week of my leave I spent a couple of days in London with a friend I had made at ITW. As someone who had very little knowledge of London, which she knew well, I enjoyed visiting historic sites and dancing at Covent Garden (ballroom not ballet) with her.

With leave over, it was up to Manchester and the usual RAF reception at Heaton Park. Heaton Park turned out to be a large collection of wartime Nissen huts spread over a large park. They were cold and draughty, so it was a bonus if you got a bed near the coke-fired stove, which was the only source of heat. Washing and toilet facilities were in separate blocks some distance away. Luckily as this was early June, going out in the mornings to wash and shave was not as arduous as it would have been in the winter.

It was crunch time for us now. What was the verdict from Grading School? A fairly large number of us were marched to a local cinema and when seated, we were briefed that we would be addressed by two officers from the platform; when our name was called, we would answer with our 'last three' (the last three digits of our service number) adding a 'Sir'. We would then be told our aircrew trade to which we would reply: 'I understand Sir'. There would be no other reply and no argument.

The names were then read out in alphabetical order. 'M' is the middle letter of the alphabet so there was a nail-biting wait before 'Markwell'. I responded 'Sir 625'. There was a pause for what felt like an eternity, followed by 'Pilot'. I responded 'I understand Sir'. The rest is a blur but there were some long faces in the audience.

Following the announcement as to our future trade, the rest of the time at ACDC was spent preparing for our overseas posting. We handed in our anti-gas capes, respirators and steel helmets and our boots were replaced with shoes. I believe that it was about this time that we removed the RAFVR badges from the shoulders of our uniforms. Then we waited for our posting. I was hoping for Canada as I had relatives out there.

During the wait we were employed on general duties. I spent time sewing grass seed around some of the huts and the rest of the time assisting in the camp training cinema. Time off was spent going into Manchester, to cinemas and dances.

Finally came the day when the postings were published. We were not told specifically where we were going but were told to mark our kitbags 'L/3'. Wartime secrecy prevented any further information being given to us but the old hands on the permanent staff said 'Convoy L3' and 'Moncton' in Canada. Just what I had hoped for.[2]

On the evening before our departure, most of us attended a communion service in the camp church. We were crossing the Atlantic and German U-boats were still active.[3]

The next morning, we loaded into trucks for Manchester Piccadilly Station and boarded a train for 'somewhere'. 'Somewhere' turned out to be Glasgow, or rather Gourock on the River Clyde. There we were loaded into a small ship (tender) and taken out to a liner lying offshore. She turned out to be the French transatlantic liner SS Île de France; any thoughts we may have had of a luxury trip were dispelled as soon as we went aboard. All her accommodation had been stripped out and she was now a troopship.

After stowing our kitbags in the hold, we went down to our troop deck; just an open deck with bars along the deck head from which we would be slinging our hammocks. Underneath the hammock bars were long wooden tables where, if the ship was full, the occupants would eat. We were lucky; the ship was

2 See *Historical Context* section, page 215, for more informaton.

3 See *Historical Context* section, page 219, for more informaton.

only lightly loaded so we were able to eat in what had been the main dining room, now strictly non-luxury. The food was cooked by the ship's civilian catering staff.

We just had a short time to try our hand at slinging a hammock taken from the pile in the deck stowage. The slinging was easy, just wrap the cords around the deck head support. The difficult part was to get into the hammock without falling out the other side which was most hilarious, and it got no easier at sea.

CANADA

JULY 1943 - DEC 1944

JULY 1943 - DEC 1944

1. MONCTON
2. BOWDEN*
3. CALGARY
4. SASKATOON*
5. MONTREAL (AND LACHINE)
6. SUMMERSIDE*
7. BOUNDARY BAY*
8. ABBOTSFORD*
9. HALIFAX
10. BANFF

* STATIONS AT WHICH ERIC SERVED

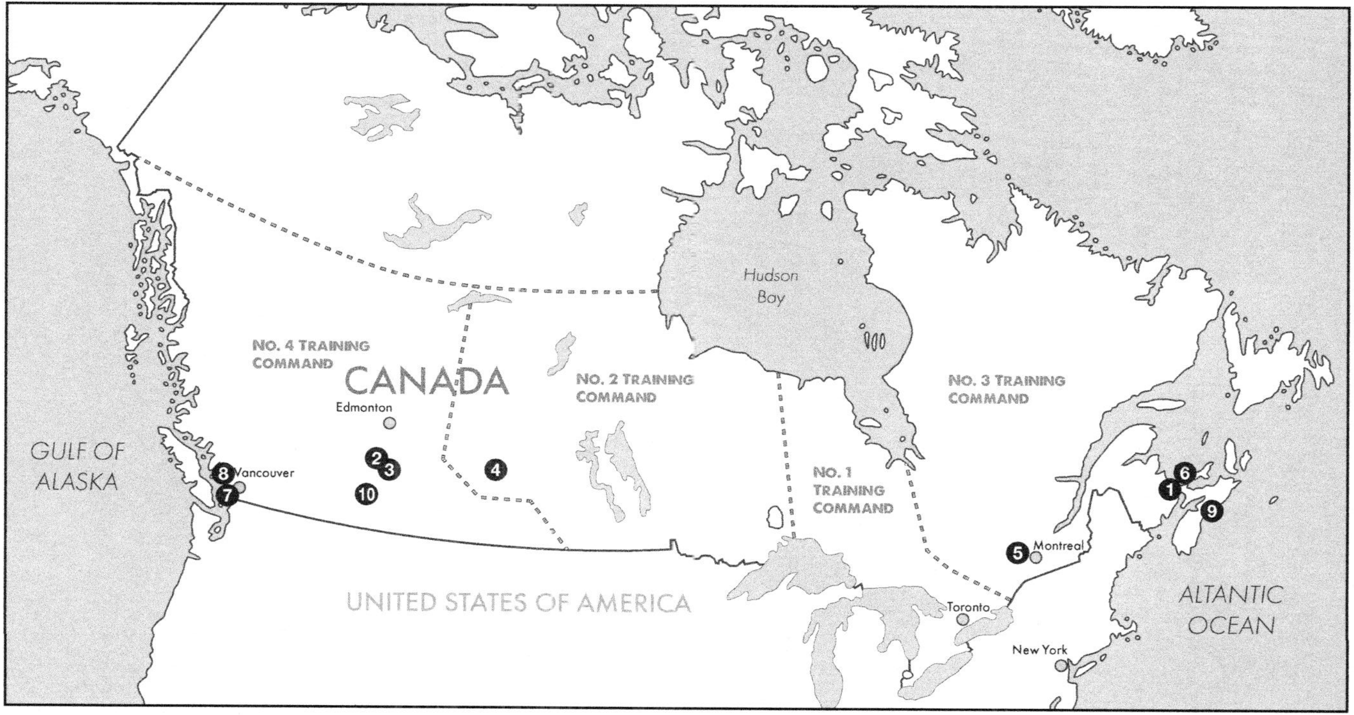

GULF OF ALASKA
No. 4 TRAINING COMMAND
CANADA
Edmonton
Vancouver
8
7
2
3
10
4
No. 2 TRAINING COMMAND
Hudson Bay
No. 1 TRAINING COMMAND
No. 3 TRAINING COMMAND
5
Montreal
Toronto
New York
6
1
9
ALTANTIC OCEAN
UNITED STATES OF AMERICA

CHAPTER 5

TRANSATLANTIC CROSSING

As we were the first draft aboard, we were detailed for guard duty at all points of entry to the ship. This lasted for two days as more drafts of RAF airmen, some soldiers and a few naval ratings came aboard. Finally came a large party of German Prisoners of War (POWs) guarded by a detachment of fully armed soldiers.

Whilst we waited on the Clyde, we saw and cheered the departure of two troopships loaded with soldiers; we wondered where they were going. Several weeks later we heard that Tunisia had been invaded (Operation Torch).

Then it was our turn to sail. My logbook doesn't give the exact date, but it was in the last days of June 1943. As soon as we were underway, it was all hands to lifeboat drill. We mustered on the main deck as directed by the crew, wearing our lifejackets which were our constant companions for the rest of the crossing. Our next shock was to be told that we would not be crossing in convoy. Apparently, it was the practice for the transatlantic liners, because they were relatively fast for ships, to cross alone. So, in late evening we passed 'Ailsa Craig' and set off into the dark.

Once the ship was underway there was no need for guards on the entry ports, so I found myself with some others in the ship's bakery, detailed to slice loaves into twelve portions for issue to the German POWs as they were not allowed to have knives. It was not a popular duty but it did have the advantage that by working with the ship's catering staff, we were not restricted to meal times and there were perks to be had in the way of a variety of foodstuffs, rather than the food served in the troop dining room. It also meant that we were excused from any other duty. Unfortunately, the knives we were using were not very sharp and after a couple of days we developed blisters on our hands.

Off duty, there was nothing to do but walk around the deck and watch the sea go by. At night of course, the ship was blacked out and it was during the evenings that the German POWs were allowed up on deck in small parties, to get some air. They were otherwise confined to the lower decks below the waterline. According to their escorts, they were all resigned to being sunk as they believed that their U-boats were sinking all Atlantic shipping.

As the voyage progressed, it became obvious from the changes in temperature, that we were not taking a direct line across the Atlantic, but were weaving north and south. We still did not know our eventual destination, but the betting was on

Halifax, Nova Scotia. On the evening of the eighth day out, there was great excitement as an aeroplane was seen approaching. It was a Liberator that circled the ship and then flew off. That was the only sign of life until the tenth morning when we saw land ahead and a few hours later passed the Statue of Liberty. We now knew where we were – New York.

Once alongside, we collected our kitbags from the hold and loaded them into buses for Grand Central Station. Having departed from battered and rationed Britain, what we saw of the city gave us the impression that we were in dreamland and Grand Central itself added to that illusion. The concourse was huge, spotlessly clean, with a huge 'Stars & Stripes' fluttering at one end in the breeze created by some concealed fans, and with much marble evident. Unlike London's main-line stations, there was no sign of any trains. Here the trains were below the concourse. Seeing all of this, it was hard to believe that the USA had been at war since 1941.

We were given a short time to walk around and take it all in; we also found that we created something of a stir with the crowds there. One very nice American couple asked me what uniform I was wearing. On being told 'RAF' they were clearly still puzzled and asked, 'What is the RAF?' 'Royal Air Force' was not much help either, until I said we were from England. That settled it and they went off happily, wishing me luck. It raised a doubt in my mind as to Americans' knowledge of the world outside the USA.

The NCOs who had met us off the ship then sent us down

to the platforms to board the train waiting there. Once aboard, off we went. The train was also a revelation; it was comfortable, but we were crowded, and it soon became hot. We did what we would have done in the UK and opened the windows, which was a mistake as soon we were covered in a thin layer of coal dust. This was of course the era of the steam train but, whereas British engines burned coal, the American ones burned pulverised coal, much of which was blown out of the smokestack.

The windows were quickly shut but it was too late; for the next twelve hours we suffered the heat and gritty coal dust until, after crossing the Canadian border to the north, we arrived at Moncton, New Brunswick. The time was 0200 hours.

Moncton was titled No. 31 Personnel Depot (PD). Despite the hour, we were documented, fed and allocated rooms in permanent blocks with all internal facilities and within an hour we had showered off all the dust and were settled for the night.

The sole function of No. 31 PD, as its title suggested, was the intake of RAF personnel, particularly trainee aircrew arriving in Canada, their dispersal westward and their eventual return to the UK. The train that had brought us was turned around and went off with a return load.

For ourselves, our time at Moncton was given over to orientation to Canada. As it was July and hot, we were issued with a lightweight tropical uniform (khaki) for summer wear. It was of a much better material than the tropical khaki uniforms issued to UK personnel, but the design was the same as our 'Blues'. Unfortunately, it had brass buttons that had to be polished - you can't have everything!

Canada also required that we be tested for susceptibility to Scarlet Fever so one of our first parades was to Sick Quarters for the 'Schick and Dick' test. The injection was under the skin of the forearm and then there was a wait of several days to see if there was a reaction. Having had the disease as a child I proved negative. Awaiting test results delayed our onward transition for a week, but in that time, we had our first pay parade with our pay in Canadian dollars. With the rate of exchange what it was then, it seemed as though we had had a pay rise - we hadn't.

The routine of the Station was quite relaxed, so we had a chance to explore the town itself. It was fairly small, but coming from a battered Britain with its blackout and severe rationing, it was quite an experience to walk around well-lit streets at night and to see the shops full of fruit, sweets and other goodies. We were also lucky to go into a restaurant and sit down to a steak that would have been a week or more rations for a large family back home, if it could be got at all.

As we were all keen to get on with our training, we found the time at No. 31 PD a bit of a drag, so there was much relief when the posting notices went up. I found myself posted to No. 32 Elementary Flying Training School (EFTS) at Bowden in Alberta, a long way from Moncton.

On the morning of 22nd July 1943 we paraded on the camp railway station to board a train for Montreal, where we would have to change Canadian railway systems. From Moncton, it would be with the Canadian National Railway (CNR) network (CNR was government owned); from Montreal we would be with the privately-owned Canadian Pacific Railway network (CPR), for the rest of our journey of some 2,000 miles.

After a not very comfortable night we arrived in Montreal, detrained and were bussed up to the CPR Windsor Station where we joined one of the cross-continental trains, being in several coaches added on to the normal train. As standard rolling stock, these coaches were full sleepers and for the next three days we lived comfortably on the train travelling through Ontario, Manitoba and Saskatchewan to Calgary in Alberta where we were uncoupled from the cross-continental and attached to a local for the rest of the sixty miles to Bowden.

Aerial photograph of No. 32 EFTS Bowden

CHAPTER 6

ELEMENTARY FLYING TRAINING (NO. 32 EFTS)

Our arrival at Bowden followed the familiar pattern of reception by the NCOs, who would be in charge of us for disciplinary purposes. They took over from the NCOs who had accompanied us across Canada, the latter returning to Moncton to wait for the next draft.

After sorting ourselves out with our kit, we were marched to our billets, henceforth referred to as our quarters. These proved to be large rooms in permanent blocks with internal toilet facilities, a far cry from the Manchester Nissen huts. Next for a meal - here at Bowden we would take our meals cafeteria style in a large airy dining room. Food was cooked and served by a mixture of service and civilian staff and was of a high standard. At Moncton, we no longer had to carry our own irons or wash them in a greasy tub of boiling water. From then on, our old irons were redundant - thank goodness! After use, the crockery and cutlery disappeared into the kitchen to reappear clean for the next meal.

The next morning, we were marched to ground school for a briefing on what to expect from the course and to complete the arrival procedure. We were told that our duty day would be split between ground school and flying, alternating weekly between mornings and afternoons.

Following the briefing we were split up into Flights. I found myself in D Flight and we were sent over to the Flights to meet our instructors. We were all delighted to see that the Tiger Moths had been replaced with the Cornell, which was a modern low wing monoplane with a totally enclosed cockpit. Even better, the trainee flew from the front cockpit, so no more having to try to see through the instructor's head.

Following an introductory talk by the Flight Commander we were introduced to our individual instructors; mine was a Flying Officer (F/O). We then went off to get our first close-up of the Cornell.

The Cornell, No. 32 EFTS Bowden.

After the Tiger Moth, it was good to see that there was full intercommunication between the front and back seats. No more shouting down a speaking tube and being unable to hear instructions properly. The instrumentation consisted of a full blind flying panel too, unlike the basics of the Tiger. The engine had an electric starter, so no more prop swinging – bliss! To complete the differences, there were hydraulic brakes incorporated in the rudder pedals, manually operated landing flaps and a tail wheel – essential as we would be flying from a hard runway, not from a grass field as we had at Southam.

After the initial introduction to the aeroplane it was back to the crew room for the issue of aeroplane notes and checklists. It was stressed upon us that checklists would not be used in the air; all drills were to be learned by heart.

That was the end of our first day of 'flying'. There was much feverish work going on in our rooms that evening; working on the various checks and fitting them into mnemonics to be used in the air.

Then began the routine working days of half ground school and half flying. In ground school, we learnt the technical aspects of the aeroplane plus all the other subjects we had covered at ITW, which we had hardly thought about since. The only subject dropped was armament. We all had to work ourselves back up to standard at Morse code, lamp and buzzer. Eventually I could read fifteen words per minute on buzzer and eight on lamp, which became useful later on.

The domestic situation at Bowden was fairly relaxed

compared with some of our previous training. Reveille was at 0600 then reporting to Flights or ground school was at 0800. The changeover came after the midday meal.

There was no working parade and whilst we were responsible for polishing the floor around our bed space and keeping it tidy, there was no laying out of kit, but the bed had to be made up. Civilian staff undertook cleaning of the ablutions.

27th July came around and I reported to D Flight for my first Cornell trip. After collecting a parachute and helmet (no other flying kit was necessary) it was out to the aeroplane for the initial familiarisation flight. This was similar to the first flight at Grading School - a look at the local area followed by 'Effects of Controls': climbing, descending, gliding and after landing, taxiing. It lasted forty-five minutes to add to the twelve hours thirty minutes already in my logbook. My first impressions were good, especially the lack of the buffeting slipstream and the good visibility from the front cockpit.

The second trip, the very next day, introduced stalling and spinning plus emergency drills. Since we had been given the grading course, we were pushed along more quickly than if we had not flown before. The third trip saw the introduction of take-off, glide approach and landing.

At this time, the RAF used the glide approach as the standard landing approach. The use of power on the approach was shown only as a demonstration before solo. Why the emphasis on glide approaches, I am not certain. We'd never use it in our later training stages; it may have

D Flight (Eric is front row, second from left).

The crucial moment!

The Cornell's 'office'.

Bowden Tigerschmitt - Tiger Moths at Bowden.
Note the cockpit canopy, a modification for the Canadian winters.

been a hangover from the biplane age, now gone.

This flight saw the introduction of the intensive circuits and landings (circuits and bumps) phase of the course, the aim being to achieve 'first solo' as soon as possible. The deadline was set at ten hours dual instruction.

Not meeting that deadline meant a 'Scrub Check'. Unless you were very lucky, this also signalled the end of pilot training and reversion to one of the other trades of Navigator or Bomb Aimer. There was therefore an element of tension in the flying.

As my hours mounted, the level of tension increased. According to the amount of criticism and sarcasm coming from the rear cockpit, it looked as though I would not make the deadline.

However, after five hours of dual flying, my Flying Officer instructor was posted to take over the navigation flight and I was handed over to a Sergeant Pilot; what a difference this made! He was quietly spoken, broke in only where necessary and instead of criticising, gave help and encouragement. After two and a half hours with him, he put me up for my solo check. With hindsight, I suspect that he had his fingers crossed; he'd had so much ground to make up in restoring my confidence. Another Sergeant Pilot carried out the solo check, but I knew when we taxied back and shut down that I hadn't made it. By this time, several of the others had gone solo, so panic definitely set in.

The next day, my patient instructor took me around the circuit for an hour but once again we taxied in and shut down.

With nine hours now gone, the future was looking bleak. Then, as we walked back to the Flight, my instructor turned to me and said: 'How would you like to go off on your own?' The answer was obvious: 'Yes please'. So I found myself walking back to the aeroplane, Cornell No. 15036.

Unusually for a first solo, I had to complete all the pre-flight and starting checks before taxiing out of dispersal. Usually the first solo came at the end of a sortie when the instructor stopped the aeroplane with the engine running, got out, secured the rear cockpit, gave a pat on the back and said: 'Off you go'.

Fortunately all went well; the circuit was reasonable, but the landing was a bit long.

My friends told me afterwards that poor Sgt. Dailey was standing out in front of the Flight (as the instructors did for all first solos), and when I came in a bit high he burst out: 'Go round'.

Then, as the aeroplane landed, surprisingly, on 'three points' (main wheels and tail wheel on the ground together) he shouted: 'Well done'. When I got back, he was waiting with a big smile and handshake. The date was 11th August 1943.

With my first solo achieved, the intensity of flying increased. In the next week, I flew eighteen hours dual and solo, consolidating what had been covered pre-solo. Dual and solo forced landings were added, as were powered approaches with some low flying (dual). At this time Sgt. Dailey went on leave and I was handed over to Sgt. Webb who remained my instructor for the rest of the course. His approach was a bit more robust than Sgt. Dailey, but we got on well.

Coincident with the flying was instrument flying training in the Link Trainer. This was the forerunner of the modern 'all-singing, all-dancing' flight simulator. It comprised a dummy cockpit on a fixed base but with the cockpit having freedom of movement in azimuth and limited movement in pitch and roll. Internally it had a full working instrument panel plus a throttle and control column to which it responded somewhat jerkily. To remove outside reference, a hinged cover covered the cockpit. Turbulence could be induced by a series of pneumatic jacks. The Link was connected by cable to a crab on the instructor's desk that followed the cockpit instruments and the instructor also had duplicate instruments.

Training on the Link was phased ahead of the flying, so that when the first dual instrument flying in the aeroplane came, at about twenty hours, we had some idea as to what it was about. For instrument flying, it was into the rear cockpit for the trainee and a canvas hood could be pulled over this cockpit to remove external reference. Unsurprisingly the aeroplane proved easier than the Trainer; it was more responsive.

At twenty-five hours came the first attempts at aerobatics; previously the instructors had flown them on some off-circuit sorties for fun, and to get us used to being upside down. Now we were shown how it should be done and got to try it for ourselves.

After two hours dual, I was sent off solo to practise aerobatics and spinning. I have to admit to some trepidation before starting and in my own mind, I felt that I would never be very good at aerobatics. Also, in this phase of the course came the Twenty-Hour Test by the Flight Commander. In fact, the test was flown at any time between twenty and thirty hours and was approached with some trepidation by us all.

Throughout my flying life I was subject to test nerves, and it lasted right to the end. Later, when I became an examiner, I found it to be very common. In the case of my Twenty-Hour Test however, all went well. Two of our course failed and were 'washed out'. That made a total of four losses to date as two others failed to make solo.

We were now halfway through the course and had our first break, a Forty-Eight Hour Pass. This was forty-eight hours in which we were free to leave the Station.

Bowden town had seven large grain elevators and little else. The other nearest town was Innisfail which was a little larger and had a dance once a week, to which some of us went once. Generally, off-duty time was limited due to the long working days and most leisure time was spent studying for the exams or in the canteen, which was large, airy and stocked many Canadian goodies, so the 'Forty-Eight' gave us a chance to explore.

Some of us went to Calgary by train, but I was luckier. One of my friends had met a farmer in Innisfail and had been entertained by the family. For the 'Forty-Eight', the farmer invited him to bring three friends for a trip into the foothills of the Rocky Mountains for a trout-fishing weekend at a cabin he had there. I was one of the party of four.

We went by car into the mountains, spent the day fishing for trout, ate what we caught, and slept the night in the cabin. The next day we went into Banff, had a swim in the hot springs and went up to Lake Louise. The large hotel at Lake Louise was closed and Banff was quiet, but the surrounding mountain scenery made our trip spectacular and unforgettable.

Two other episodes in the early part of the course that left unhappy memories were two fatal accidents. They both happened to the senior course; there were two courses training at Bowden of which we were the junior. As junior course, we were detailed to provide the firing party of eight. We were paraded and our rifle drill was checked; as a result, I found myself in the firing party at the gravesides where we fired the three volleys. These accidents cast a shadow over the Station for a while but with the intensity of training, they soon slipped into the past.

After the 'Forty-Eight' it was back to the grindstone and some thirty-five hours flying, including four hours instrument time. The next hurdle was night flying. For this, we flew with instructors from one of the other Flights. There was a reason for this, which I can't remember, but I flew with three separate instructors to complete the necessary four hours dual. Somewhat to my surprise, night flying proved to be no problem and I went solo after three hours dual. Unfortunately, our night flying was somewhat protracted due to a number of prairie thunderstorms which could arrive very quickly and be very active. In fact, on one of my day solo off-circuit sorties I got cut off from base by an unexpected storm and had to land at the reserve landing ground south of Bowden and sit out the storm.

Apart from these thunderstorms (this was the height of the Canadian summer), there was very little delay to the course. Flying started at 0600 hours and went on until 2000 or later, if night flying was scheduled. When we were on the early shift, we were awakened at 0500.

Along with the flying was the continuation of ground school lectures, which involved some evenings spent revising for the end of course exams. This was not easy after an 0500 start and often four sorties dual and/or solo per day, but the work had to be done. The exams duly came and went, all of which were comfortably passed.

It was now early September and the course had only three weeks to run, so the flying intensity increased further. First came pilot navigation, with the navigation flight. Here I again encountered my F/O ex-instructor for two of the three dual sorties. These must have gone well as I was cleared for solo navigation and went off two days later, on a two-hour sortie. This was followed, after another dual trip with another instructor, by a 'land-away' to DeWinton another EFTS near Calgary. Each leg took one hour thirty minutes. That completed the navigation syllabus.

Between the navigation trips were further dual and solo handling flights and a test by an examiner from the Empire

Central Flying School (ECFS). ECFS was tasked with maintaining flying standards throughout the Empire Air Training Scheme by visiting all of the schools involved. It carried out tests of instructors rather more than trainees, on a random basis. The only comment I got from the examiner was a query as to why I had not used full landing flap for landing. The answer was easy, we were not taught to do so. That would certainly have come up on discussion with the instructors.

With the end of the course now approaching, the emphasis was on instrument flying both in the Link and in the air, in preparation for the Instrument Test. That went well as did the Forty-Five Hour Test with the Flight Commander, but on the Final Test, taken on the same day with another Flight Commander I hiccupped on the precautionary landing, so had to sweat out that night to await the verdict. The next morning Sgt. Webb took me on a session of precautionary landings at the conclusion of which he said: 'OK, you've passed'. Much relief and joy!

The final ten days at Bowden were devoted to a revision of all the handling exercises and completion of the instrument syllabus.

It was now time to think of the next posting. I was fairly sure that I would not be going on to a single engine Service Flying Training School (SFTS). My aerobatics were not particularly good whereas my instrument flying was. This assumption proved correct, as when the posting notice went up on the notice board, I found my destination to be No. 4 SFTS at Saskatoon, a twin-engine school.

The surprise was the destination; most postings from Bowden were to RAF SFTSs. No. 4 SFTS was a Royal Canadian Air Force (RCAF) unit. However, twenty-one of us were going there, an unusual posting from Bowden.

Our last action at Bowden was to hand in our summer uniform as it was unlikely that we would be in Canada the following summer.

At Bowden, we had completed seventy-three hours flying dual and solo. I came away assessed as 'Average' with a mark of 69.7%.

Course 86, No. 32 EFTS Bowden.
Eric is front row, 6th from the right.

CHAPTER 7

SERVICE FLYING TRAINING (NO. 4 SFTS)

The journey between Bowden and Saskatoon involved a change of train at Calgary from the CPR to the CNR, as Saskatoon was served only by the CNR. Arrival at 'No. 4' as we came to call it, was late in the evening so we were pointed in the direction of our quarters and left to our own devices for the night.

Our barrack block was known as the 'Double Decker'. It was the only two-storey building on the Station and housed all the trainee pilots in four rooms, two up and two down. In the rooms we occupied two-tier bunks with lockers above them. I drew a lower bunk and above me was the oldest trainee of us all. He was twenty-seven and usually referred to as 'Dad' for obvious reasons as most of us had just had our twentieth birthdays.

The next morning, following the working parade, we were

marched up to the ground school for the usual administration and briefing on the Station and the course. We found that our course was composed of we twenty-one RAF and thirty-two RCAF trainees. We would be split into two sections, Red and Blue, each with a mix of RAF and RCAF personnel. For some reason I never understood, I found myself Section Leader of Red Section. I found that it entailed quite a lot of extra duties but probably paid off in the end.

Once sorted out administratively, the next stop was the hangar where our Flight was located. I found myself in C Flight and that my instructor would be P/O Barber, who would have four trainees, two RAF and two RCAF. My co-trainee would be Eric 'Mac' MacLellan who hailed from Glasgow. We became good friends and kept in touch for some time after the war. We also found that the aeroplane we would be flying would be the Cessna Crane, not as was usual in the RAF SFTSs, where the aeroplane was either the Airspeed Oxford or the Avro Anson.

Most of us had hoped for the Oxford, which was reputed to be the better of the two, so we viewed the Crane with some suspicion at first, but grew to like it as we progressed. The instruction staff were all RCAF, we were the only RAF personnel on the Station, but we were told that this was not unusual; there had been RAF trainees on previous courses.

On 23rd September 1943, I had my initial familiarisation flight in Crane 1a FJ 249 with P/O Barber. This was the usual first trip in a new aeroplane and followed a familiar pattern of looking at the local area and carrying out some handling to get

Eric at No. 4 SFTS Saskatoon.

Cessna Crane echelon port,
No. 4 SFTS Saskatoon.

Eric captioned this 'Cool Pilot'!

Avro Anson, No. 4 SFTS Saskatoon.

Eric, with a Cessna Crane, No. 4 SFTS.

Eric with Bob Tait Nov '43.

the feel of the controls, which of course felt much different from the aeroplanes we had flown before. What was also different, because the Crane had a double seat behind the operating pilots, was that another trainee could be carried to observe the exercise being demonstrated and also to change seats in the air in order to repeat the exercise without having to land.

There was much to learn on our introduction to the new aeroplane. Apart from its size, there were two of everything: throttles, propeller controls (as it had constant speed propellers), mixture levers and carburettor heat controls, plus of course two sets of engine instruments.

The blind flying panel was also different. We were used to the standard RAF six instrument panel, common to all RAF aeroplanes, but here we had an American aeroplane with the instruments across the top of the panel in a haphazard pattern.

On the next sortie on the same day from No. 4, Mac my co-trainee and I climbed aboard Crane 1a FJ 249 and P/O Barber took off for the No. 2 Reserve landing field at Osler. Unusually, once there, one of us got out and the other went off for a dual handling exercise that also covered some emergencies, then it was the turn of the other to repeat the exercise. On the ground again, it was both on board for Saskatoon.

The next sortie repeated the pattern, concentrating on circuits and bumps at Osler, which was a grass field, before returning to base. The third sortie introduced asymmetric flying on the ferry flight to and from base and the fourth and fifth sorties repeated the pattern with asymmetric circuits and landings thrown in.

After six and a half hours flying, I was put up for solo and after a thirty-minute check, went solo at Osler. After the solo, the return flight to base saw the initial introduction to instrument flying followed the next day by the introduction to navigation with two map-reading sorties in the Anson 2 – another type which was to re-appear later in the course. It was all go.

Co-incident with the flying was Link training and ground school lectures in all the usual subjects, with particular emphasis on meteorology applicable to the locality. With our course scheduled to go through the winter, it was considered essential that we were aware of how rapidly the weather could change and how severe it could be on the prairies.

A period of solo consolidation followed. This included solo asymmetric landings, both at Osler and on the hard runways at Saskatoon. Interspersed with the solo were some instrument flying (dual) and an introduction to the Crane 1, which had a completely different cockpit layout to the 1a but had the standard blind flying panel and some more pilot navigation. The Anson navigation flights were flown as Navigator.

This pattern of flying continued on an almost daily basis until the end of October, when I found myself flying with the Chief Flying Instructor (CFI) on a Progress Check. Again, my fear of tests took over and things were not going too well when we ran into a snowstorm. The CFI so enjoyed showing me how to find base in the storm that he forgot about my errors. I was saved again!

In early November, with sixty hours of the course gone, it was time for night flying. Two hours dual was followed by solo and after two hours solo on the circuit, it was off on night cross-countries. Two hours were flown dual, then it was back to the circuit to complete five hours solo, added to the seven hours dual, giving us twelve hours at night. The night flying took up most of November.

In tandem with this flying, we were now learning procedural instrument flying on the Link, working up to carrying out simulated Standard Beam Approaches (SBA). SBA was the only instrument landing system in this era. There were let-down procedures using radio ranges that we also practised in the Link, but they were not landing aids.

After night flying came bombing training, using the camera obscura as the target. This entailed positioning the aeroplane a certain distance out from the target, flying on a heading at right angles to it, calculating the heading to track over the target. As one turned on to the bombing run, one would call 'attack, attack' on the radio, hoping to arrive overhead the target after a given timed run.

Since we had little forward view of the target as we ran in, it was a 'fingers crossed' exercise but surprisingly it usually worked. The bombing took about eighteen hours dual and solo and interspersed with this were two long solo cross-countries each of three hours.

These activities had taken us well into December and the heavy snow had arrived. This was a new experience as no attempt was made to clear the snow from the runways. It was rolled and the edges of the runways marked with cones. The cold also hit, with temperatures well below zero all the time. The intense cold meant that the aeroplanes had to be put into the hangars overnight and started up immediately when they were rolled out in the mornings.

We had been issued with cold weather headgear and overshoes for use in the snow when on the ground. In the air, the aeroplane heating system was efficient enough for us not to need any heavy flying clothing; battledress was sufficient.

In the middle of December came the final Instrument Test and Link SBA Test. I negotiated both safely. We then had the first interruption to our training from the weather and we did not fly for a week. It was then Christmas and the Station shut down for five days.

Over Christmas a friend of mine from EFTS who had been posted to North Battleford, an RAF SFTS to the north of Saskatoon, came down with some others to see Saskatoon. They had booked into a local hotel and invited me to join them.

On Christmas Eve we went to the Bessborough for a good meal - a CPR hotel and the best in town. On Christmas Day we were invited to join a local family for the day. It was a pleasant interlude and an opportunity to exchange news with the others from Bowden. After Boxing Day, they returned to North Battleford and I went back to No. 4.

Cessna Crane, No. 4 SFTS, Saskatoon.

Just one flare!

Having been at No. 4 since September, we had seen the daylight decreasing which, of course, reduced the flying day and gave us more leisure time in the evenings. The Station had a 'Duty Watch' scheme that entailed 50% of personnel being on the Station at all times. The duty was changed every day and there was a roll call at 1800 every evening. It involved a lot of people and was rather resented, so often when one of us had a reason for going into town we would ask our friends to cover for us. This was fine; someone in the rear rank would answer for whoever was missing. That produced the odd hiccup when two or more friends answered. However, the NCOs calling the roll never batted an eyelid; they weren't too keen on being kept on camp either.

Off duty there was quite a lot of entertainment in Saskatoon, which had two cinemas and there were dances most nights, run by local organisations such as the Canadian Legion. Also, as with anywhere in Canada, there were plenty of restaurants where one could have a good steak or other meal. The problem of course was the limit to which our pay would stretch. On camp, there was also a cinema, a good canteen and if one was invited, the Women's Division (WD) canteen, where there was usually dancing to the Jukebox.

On 29th December flying started again, this time on the Anson 2, to fly the SBA for real. This lasted a week and involved nine hours in all. After that it was back to the Crane for more navigation - dual and solo with some handling refresher flying as well.

With ground school exams having been taken and passed before Christmas, it was now all flying. We were detached to the relief landing ground at Vanscoy. This was not very popular as it meant that for the next two weeks we would be away from the entertainments of Saskatoon.

The rationale behind the move was that with a new course starting at No. 4 and having the airfield at Vanscoy to ourselves, we could concentrate on flying unhindered. The accommodation was permanent, much as at Saskatoon, so it was comfortable but isolated. The instructors also disliked being away from home; most of them lived off camp in Saskatoon.

Now the emphasis switched to formation flying which was flown dual and solo and finally amounted to a total of fifteen hours.

With formation completed it was back to refresher flying for the real 'crunch'; the Wings Test was looming. To date all of the RAF trainees had survived the course, but in the other half of the course, two of the Canadians had been 'washed out'.

On 6th January 1944 came my turn with the CFI. One hour thirty minutes later we were back on the ground. The instructor turned to me, shook my hand and said, 'well done!' I had passed - celebrations all round!

In the next few days all of us passed. Few of us drank alcohol at that time so we celebrated with orange squash.

With the major hurdle crossed, the rest was something of an anti-climax for me. Some fifteen hours of flying were necessary

No. 4 SFTS Saskatoon Red Section Course 90 (Sept 1943 - Feb 1944). Eric can be seen back row, extreme left.

CANADA - ENGLAND - U.S.A.

WINGS GRADUATION DINNER

COURSE 90

No. 4 Service Flying Training School

THE BESSBOROUGH
Saskatoon, Saskatchewan
Canada

THURSDAY, FEBRUARY 10th
1944

No. 4 SFTS Saskatoon Red Section Course 90 (Sept 1943 - Feb 1944).

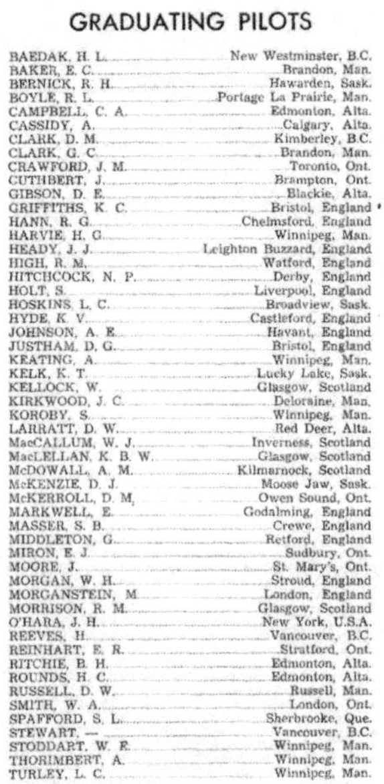

GRADUATING PILOTS

BAEDAK, H. L.	New Westminster, B.C.
BAKER, E. C.	Brandon, Man.
BERNICK, R. H.	Hawarden, Sask.
BOYLE, R. L.	Portage La Prairie, Man.
CAMPBELL, C. A.	Edmonton, Alta.
CASSIDY, A.	Calgary, Alta.
CLARK, D. M.	Kimberley, B.C.
CLARK, G. C.	Brandon, Man.
CRAWFORD, J. M.	Toronto, Ont.
CUTHBERT, J.	Brampton, Ont.
GIBSON, D. E.	Blackie, Alta.
GRIFFITHS, K. C.	Bristol, England
HANN, R. G.	Chelmsford, England
HARVIE, H. G.	Winnipeg, Man.
HEADY, J. J.	Leighton Buzzard, England
HIGH, R. M.	Watford, England
HITCHCOCK, N. P.	Derby, England
HOLT, S.	Liverpool, England
HOSKINS, L. C.	Broadview, Sask.
HYDE, K. V.	Castleford, England
JOHNSON, A. E.	Havant, England
JUSTHAM, D. G.	Bristol, England
KEATING, A.	Winnipeg, Man.
KELK, K. T.	Lucky Lake, Sask.
KELLOCK, W.	Glasgow, Scotland
KIRKWOOD, J. C.	Deloraine, Man.
KOROBY, S.	Winnipeg, Man.
LARRATT, D. W.	Red Deer, Alta.
MacCALLUM, W. J.	Inverness, Scotland
MacLELLAN, K. B. W.	Glasgow, Scotland
McDOWALL, A. M.	Kilmarnock, Scotland
McKENZIE, D. J.	Moose Jaw, Sask.
McKERROLL, D. M.	Owen Sound, Ont.
MARKWELL, E.	Godalming, England
MASSER, S. B.	Crewe, England
MIDDLETON, G.	Retford, England
MIRON, E. J.	Sudbury, Ont.
MOORE, J.	St. Mary's, Ont.
MORGAN, W. H.	Stroud, England
MORGANSTEIN, M.	London, England
MORRISON, R. M.	Glasgow, Scotland
O'HARA, J. H.	New York, U.S.A.
REEVES, H.	Vancouver, B.C.
REINHART, E. R.	Stratford, Ont.
RITCHIE, B. H.	Edmonton, Alta.
ROUNDS, H. C.	Edmonton, Alta.
RUSSELL, D. W.	Russell, Man.
SMITH, W. A.	London, Ont.
SPAFFORD, S. L.	Sherbrooke, Que.
STEWART, —	Vancouver, B.C.
STODDART, W. E.	Winnipeg, Man.
THORIMBERT, A.	Winnipeg, Man.
TURLEY, L. C.	Winnipeg, Man.

No. 4 SFTS Saskatoon Red Section Course 90 (Sept 1943 - Feb 1944).

to complete the syllabus comprising: general handling, two solo reconnaissance sorties, a solo to local towns, a further three hours of SBA at night in the Anson, and the last of the instrument flying.

During the last week of the course, two important lists were posted on the notice board - the postings and the promotions. It was known that most of the Canadians would be commissioned and it was estimated that, on past form, some 33% of we RAF trainees would be commissioned. With twenty-one of us on the course, that equated to seven and when the list was published, that was confirmed, there were seven names on the list. Most names were as expected but I was very surprised and obviously delighted that mine was one of them.

The rest of the course was promoted to Sergeant Pilot. These promotions were dated to take effect on 11th February 1944, the date set for our 'Wings Parade'. Of the Canadians, twenty-eight of thirty were commissioned; we were quite sorry for the two who missed out.

The other list gave the postings; eighteen of the twenty-one of us were going back to Moncton, bound for home, but three of us, myself included, were going to General Reconnaissance Schools (GRS) on Prince Edward Island (PEI) in Eastern Canada to do the course for eventual posting to Coastal Command. I was to go to No. 2 GRS at Summerside and the other two would go to Charlottetown to No. 1 GRS. We were three of the seven 'officers to be'.

We also received our logbook assessments. To my surprise mine read:

> *'As a T/E Pilot – Above the Average*
> *In Navigation - Average*
> *In Bombing - Exceptional*
> *Comments - No outstanding faults*
> *(11th Feb 1944)'*

During the last week of the course there was considerable activity away from flying. I found myself as Section Leader visiting all parts of the Station, clutching a bunch of clearance chits for my section. These had to be signed at each component part of the unit, to indicate that there was no charge or loaned equipment outstanding against any individual before they could leave No. 4. It proved a tiresome and frustrating duty.

Additionally, we formed a small committee in Red Section to design and have made a souvenir pennant, for presentation to our instructors, to join other mementoes of previous courses hanging in their crew room. The final design had our course number (90) in the centre with all the names of Red Section, Canadian and RAF, woven around it. It was made for us by a shop in town, was duly presented to the Flight Commander and much admired. There was also a committee, formed from both sections, to organise our Graduation Dinner and Graduation Ball.

On the night of 10th February 1944, we assembled at the Bessborough hotel together with our instructors, Station Commander, CFI and Link instructors for the formal

Graduation Dinner where toasts were drunk to Canada, His Majesty the King and the Service. It was a great way to celebrate the end of the course.

With dinner over, the Graduation Ball followed. Graduation Balls were the highlight of the year for many on the Station; the instructors brought along their wives and the Canadian graduates brought along their girlfriends.

I was told that there was much envy among the WDs of those girls invited to partner RAF 'exiles'. It ended fairly late then we were all bussed back to camp to prepare for the 'great day'.

The morning of 11th February was given over to cleaning buttons and shoes and pressing uniforms for the afternoon parade, also to packing our kit. At 1400 we assembled for our Graduation Parade. As the snow was still on the ground and the temperature was below freezing, it was to be held in the hangar.

The rest of the Station was paraded to form three sides of a square, with the front open. In front of them were the guests, officers and wives of the Station. They were all wearing greatcoats as it was very cold, but we fell in outside the hangar without greatcoats for obvious reasons. Having been sorted into alphabetical order, we were marched into the hangar to form the fourth side of the square. As the Warrant Officer (pilot in charge) said, 'plenty of swagger chaps' – there was!

Halted in front of the audience, the Station Commander gave a few words of introduction and then it was the presentation.

As the first name was called, he came to attention, marched to the centre of the Flight, turned to face the CO, marched three paces forward, saluted and received his Wings. As he did so the second recipient followed the same sequence but halted until the man in front, having received his Wings, stepped back two paces, saluted and turned to march to the back of the Flight. The second recipient then took his three paces forward and so it went on, until it was my turn.

As the CO pinned on the Wings, he said a word or two, shook my hand and then it was step back, salute and retire. It was a memorable moment for all of us; seventeen months of hard work and worry were over. We were Pilots.

Following the parade, there was a course photograph and then, at the invitation of P/O Barber, whose four pupils had been commissioned, our first visit to the Officers' Mess for a celebration with him and his wife. Afterwards it was back to our room to sew on the Wings and finish packing.

The next day, the people going to Moncton left by train in the morning, with the officers still in Airmen's uniform but wearing white armbands which they would retain until they reached the UK, when they would be kitted out correctly.

For the three of us staying in Canada it was different. We had fourteen days leave before reporting to the GRSs, so we left the camp for a local hotel and set about getting ourselves uniforms. This proved no problem; the local tailors were used to it and by the end of the day we were all fitted with new uniforms with a thin blue stripe on the sleeve. One of us, Dave, had relatives in the USA so he elected to go and visit them. Maurice and I decided to stay in Saskatoon for a week, as we knew some local people; we would then head east.

This also gave us a chance to return any unwanted kit to No. 4, to be issued with a new identity card and draw an advance of pay. As we were now earning seventeen shillings, sixpence (eighty-seven and a half pence) per day, we felt rich. It enabled us to enjoy our week's leave.

After our week of relaxation, we took the train east. I planned to stay a day or two in Montreal to meet relatives, an uncle, aunt and cousin that I had never met before. Despite this, when my uncle met me at the platform barrier, I immediately recognised him. He was my father's brother and the likeness was very obvious. I stayed with them for three days, during which time my cousin, a teacher in one of the high schools, showed me much of Montreal. It was a beautiful city with much of its architecture derived from France, the province of Quebec having been the centre of what had been French Canada.

No. 4 SFTS Saskatoon Graduation Day, 11th February 1944 (Eric is 2nd row, third from left).

CHAPTER 8

GENERAL RECONNAISSANCE SCHOOL (NO. 1 GRS)

The journey from Montreal to Summerside was another by overnight sleeper, made more interesting because when we arrived at the coast of New Brunswick, just north of Moncton, we did not have to leave the train for the crossing to Prince Edward Island. The train was shunted onto a railway ferry for the crossing and once across, shunted back onto the rail track; the first stop was Summerside.

There were a number of RCAF officers on the train, all bound, as was I, for No. 1 GRS. We were collected from the station by bus and when we arrived at the camp were shown to our quarters – barrack rooms again! The difference this time was that we had a double tier bunk to ourselves (no 'top berther') and we had the full use of the Officers' Mess. In our rooms, we were just required to make our beds, all other chores were carried out by civilian staff.

When the course assembled the next morning, I found that there were only three of us from the RAF, the rest were RCAF. I was paired up to work with one of the other RAF officers. All of us on the course were recent graduates, all pilots.

The course leader who briefed us was an RCAF Pilot, a Flight Lieutenant, who had done a tour of operations in Coastal Command and returning to Canada, had drawn the job of turning us into navigators within two months.

The course would comprise all navigator work, building upon the basics we had learned during our pilot training and covering all the skills needed to navigate an aeroplane accurately and safely when needed. The rationale, the instructor (Mac from now on), explained, was because Coastal Command carried only one navigator in the aeroplane and flew very long patrols. The navigation of the aeroplane in the patrol phases was shared between the pilots and navigator to reduce fatigue. The actual flying of the aeroplane was also shared between the pilots and the automatic pilot (if working!).

Mac also went on to explain the way we would work. We would work with him in the classroom on basic practices, such as dead reckoning and wind finding. We would carry out the necessary plotting work under his supervision and then we would fly the exercise twice, once as Navigator with the other member of the pair assisting and then switch roles on the second flight.

Our aeroplane, the Anson 5, would be flown by Staff Pilots and not by us. As the course progressed, we were introduced to more and more advanced navigation skills, including the use of the sextant, to give us sun and star position lines to use for position fixing. This was a tedious procedure, but with nothing else available these procedures were necessary; radio aids were limited to position lines from bearings obtained by the radio operator if in range and the equipment was working. In some later exercises we did 'shoot' the sun and used the sun compass extensively, if the sun happened to be shining. We did no night flying, so the star shots were made from within a particular classroom, equipped with a dozen astrodomes. The results were logged in a Star Sight Diary and submitted for checking. We were required to submit sixty sights during the course. With the calculations and plotting involved, this meant a number of nights in the Astro classroom, taking the shots.

As our skills improved, we moved on to more complicated navigation exercises covering the several types of patrols and searches used by Coastal Command with each airborne exercise being marked by Mac.

Navigation was not the only subject studied at GRS. We also received instruction in ship recognition, both naval and merchant, Allied and enemy. The recognition room contained scale models of some 170 ships, and we were expected to be able to recognise them all. For the merchant ships, it was only necessary to estimate the tonnage, but the naval ships had to be known. They included all the major capital ships of Britain, USA, Germany, Italy and Japan. For the smaller ships, it was only necessary to know the class e.g. 'Destroyer, J to R Class'.

The instructor pointed out the peculiarities of each then they were placed on a moving belt above the display to give us a varied aspect of each to commit to memory. Many of our free evenings were spent in the ship recognition room.

Navigation and ship recognition were the main subjects on the course, but we also came up against our old friend the Morse code; this time, reading the lamp rather than the buzzer as this was the main communicating medium on convoy patrol.

Late in the course came the final navigation test on the 'Tactical Floor', where we sat in a cubicle, navigating a simulated aeroplane from a shore base to intercept a convoy. To make it more difficult we were working against a clock running at double speed. Outbound we were given drifts so that we could calculate winds and apply them to maintain our track to the convoy, using standard Coastal Command navigation drill. At the time we estimated that we should see the convoy, we would open a shutter in front of us and hopefully, there it was - too bad if it wasn't. The directing staff that had been looking over our shoulders would not allow the shutter to be opened if you had made an error. You then had to set up a search pattern to find the convoy.

I found mine where it should have been and promptly received a Morse message on lamp from the Commodore, setting me off on a specific pattern patrol to investigate a possible 'contact'. At the end of the 'negative' patrol, it was back to the convoy, which of course had moved on - another navigation problem to solve. Once found, the lamp signalled a return to base, to much relief as that ended the exercise. Considering that it was the era before the advent of modern simulators, this was a well set-up exercise and really stretched us.

Coming towards the end of the course, we combined navigation and ship recognition to carry out a reconnaissance flight to the harbours of Halifax and St. John to report on the shipping there, producing 'recce' reports of what we saw. Then followed two flights carrying out specific search patterns that were not pre-planned. With these, when we were airborne, the Pilot produced the instruction for the patrol on what we thought was a normal out and back sortie. Frantic work by the Navigator followed but all went well for my flying partner and I. The final flight on the course involved a fairly complicated trip with Mac on board. After landing if he said 'ok' you had passed; we did.

The final test of ship recognition involved the recognition of fifty ships, placed on the moving belt at the top of the model display. This gave a time of approximately thirty seconds to identify each ship. I can't remember the pass mark, but one of the other RAF pilots and I got 100%. Previous to our course, this would have meant that we would have been retained at Summerside to teach ship recognition to the next intake. In our case this was not to be; having passed all aspects of the course, we were posted back to Moncton for onward movement to the UK.

During our time at Summerside, I had got to know many of the RCAF officers on the course and thoroughly enjoyed

Eric with an Anson at Summerside.

Old Faithful - Station Hack.

their company. In fact, on the few chances we had to visit Summerside town, the heavy snow of winter having gradually dissipated with the advent of spring, they were my companions and we enjoyed exploring the town together, also, in the room we shared, we mixed well. One of them had brought his trumpet; he was a good player and we enjoyed many sessions of the latest hit numbers from him. My logbook carries many of their signatures and comments, all valued mementoes of a hard course enlivened by good companions.

At the end of the course we were presented with our Air Navigator's Certificate, Second Class by the Station Commander and it was then time to leave for Moncton.

We left Summerside at the end of April 1944 expecting to spend a short time at Moncton and then be shipped home, but when we arrived at Moncton, we found that there was a hold-up in the shipping. The reason was obscure but became obvious later. I was re-united with my friends Dave and Maurice who had finished their course at Charlottetown. We had now been together since ITW and would stay together for some time to come until tragedy struck at a future date.

Time dragged at Moncton as we had no specific duties, although we did have the use of a Link Trainer. We spent some time refreshing our instrument flying and being introduced to some further instrument procedures such as Radio Range (Eric's logbook shows five hours thirty minutes on the Link). To get us away and, I suspect, out of their hair, the Station Adjutant offered us fourteen days leave. Dave went off to the United States again, Maurice went back to Saskatoon and I, having heard that its famous stampede was imminent, went off to Calgary where I spent the week watching the parades of indigenous North Americans through the town. I also went to the stadium to watch all the contests of cowboy skills and the very exciting Chuck Wagon racing. Calgary was very much in carnival spirit. Getting there had, of course, been by sleeper train and constituted my third trip across Canada. With the stampede over, I went to join Maurice in Saskatoon and we travelled back to Moncton together - my fourth trip across Canada.

In Calgary I had stayed with a family whose address I had got from the YMCA. Throughout our time in wartime Canada we found that the YMCA had a list of families offering hospitality to British servicemen. I already had a 'family' in Saskatoon and later was to find one in Vancouver.

On 6th June, back again at Moncton, we were sitting in the Officers' Mess at lunchtime, listening to one officer, a good pianist, playing the Warsaw Concerto. Someone switched on the radio and we heard that the invasion of Europe had started. Now we knew why there was no shipping to take us home - an historic moment.

Further time drifted by and still there were no ships; it was frustrating to say the least. Then one day we were called by the Adjutant. Apparently the Transport Command Operational Training Unit (OTU) at Comox on Vancouver Island had vacancies for pilots to train on the Dakota there. Were we interested? We certainly were! The three of us, accompanied now by Sandy Lockyer, who had been my 'pair' at Summerside, set out for Comox.

Sandy Lockyer. The photo is signed 'The Very Best of Luck 26.4.44'.

Having fourteen days to get there, we planned to spend a few days in Saskatoon on the way, to see if we could scrounge a flight or so from our old instructors and renew our contacts there. Sandy, although trained at North Battleford, had arranged for a friend to meet him in Saskatoon. Once there we went up to No. 4 and were each able to scrounge a flight. I flew again with my instructor Fred Barber who had been promoted to Flying Officer. Since it was now five months since we had flown, the experience was sobering – we had lost our touch.

Our hopes of getting some more flying were dashed abruptly by receipt of a signal message from Moncton recalling us immediately; our posting was cancelled. Why, we never discovered. So, back on to the train again eastbound – my sixth trip across Canada.

It was now July - we had been at Moncton for two and a half months when again came the summons. There was a Liberator

OTU at Boundary Bay, on the west coast, which wanted Second Pilots. Coastal Command flew Liberators, we were Coastal trained, ergo that must be for us. Only too glad to get going, we agreed. So, once more it was on the train, this time right across Canada to Vancouver, changing at Montreal, a full five days on the train.

CHAPTER 9

OPERATIONAL TRAINING UNIT (NO. 5 OTU)

Arriving at Vancouver at the end of July 1944, we were met and taken to No. 5 OTU at Boundary Bay, some distance from the city and located, just as the name implied, on a bay on the Canada/USA international boundary. Once again, our quarters were barrack rooms like Summerside, with us each having a two-tier bunk for our sole use.

Settling in, we found that our roommates were a mixture of aircrew trades and that the Station was a bomber OTU with crews destined for the Far East bomber squadrons. We also found that we would be flying the North American Mitchell aeroplane at Boundary, before posting to Abbotsford to fly the Liberator. Also, we would not have use of the Officers' Mess but would have a separate Aircrew Mess, which would be shared with NCO aircrew. The reason behind this policy was that we would get to know the other aircrew trades, officers and NCOs and, by mutual agreement, end up forming crews. It seemed a haphazard system but there was nothing else suggested so we had to give it a try.

In my case, there was a Pilot two beds down from me who was posted in as a Captain. After a few days settling in and technical lectures on the aeroplane, he asked me if I would join him as Second Pilot; I said yes. He then suggested I should undertake to find the rest of the crew.

The Navigator came next; he happened to be in the bed next to me. He agreed to join us and suggested a Bomb Aimer whom he knew; that made up the nucleus of a crew for the Mitchell. We would pick up the other seven crew members when we moved on to Abbotsford for Liberator conversion. For the record, we were Tom (Captain), myself (Second Pilot), Johnny (Navigator) and Ray (Bomb Aimer).

Before we started flying there was a spell in the classroom, to learn the technical details and drills for the Mitchell and its engines (Wright Cyclones). It was naturally more complicated than anything we had handled so far. Whilst Tom and I were involved in this, Johnny and Ray were getting used to working together in the navigation section. They would not join us until the end of the Captain's conversion about a month later.

As Second Pilot I was only given five hours handling on the Mitchell and spent quite a lot of time sitting in the back whilst the conversion, day and night, was completed. I only got to act as Second Pilot for the Captain's solo sorties. I did manage to get quite a lot of instrument practice in the Link during this time and also flew a five-hour sortie in the Celestial Navigation Trainer, with Johnny and Ray working together on an Astro exercise, but overall, I found it rather boring. Obviously, bomber Second Pilots were not used in the same way as in Coastal, but we were committed.

In the last week at Boundary, we flew together as a crew, carrying out four sorties, two cross-countries and two bombing. That completed twenty-six hours for me but forty for the Captain.

During the early days at Boundary, I went into Vancouver with two friends, both navigators. We visited the YMCA to see if there were any families offering hospitality to servicemen. We were sent out to a house on Point Grey, as the people there had offered to accommodate three. When we got there, we found the owner was a widowed lady. Her daughter also lived there, but she was able to offer two rooms; the next-door neighbours had room for one.

Since the navigators were long-time friends, it was logical that I go next door. This I did and found an elderly couple who welcomed me in, showed me the room and intimated that I was free to come and go at any time, and to consider it my home whilst in Vancouver. Their garden sloped down into the bay and there was a sailing dinghy tied up there that belonged to their son who was away at university. The only thing I was asked was that I get a liquor licence. Canada had very strict laws on the sale of liquor and if I did not want it myself, the husband would like it to take with him to the Vancouver Yacht

Course 8, No. 5 OTU Boundary Bay, Eric is middle row second from right. Courtesy/via Michael DesMazes.

Liberator EW218 'U' and Mitchell HD335 'V' (background, right) both flown by Eric during his time at Boundary Bay, courtesy Howell Image, DesMazes collection.

Mitchell cockpit - OTU Boundary Bay.

Mitchell at Boundary Bay.

Liberator cockpit, Boundary Bay.

Liberators, OTU Boundary Bay.

Mitchells and Liberators, on the Boundary Bay flight line.
(Image copyright: RCAF)

Club, where he was a member. It was a small price to pay for what literally became my off-duty home for the next three months. They were the Eakins family. I shall always remember their kindness.

After the early trips into Vancouver and realising that we should want to go there often during our course but not necessarily at times when there was transport available, someone suggested that we club together and buy a car, selling it again at the end of the course. The outcome was that six of us did just that. Unfortunately, only one of the group could drive, which was soon remedied.

We drove around the local area with him, and when he said we were ok, presented ourselves one by one, to the Vancouver police to take a driving test. Surprisingly we all passed and received our British Columbia (BC) driving licences. After that, when we wanted to go into Vancouver, off we went. The arrangement worked well and there was never any friction over who should have the car as generally when one of us wanted it, it was available.

It was now time to move over to Abbotsford to tackle the Liberator. We found exactly the same accommodation plan there, barrack blocks and an Aircrew Mess only, although much bigger, as we were now joined by a large number of Wireless Operators/Air Gunners (W/Op/AGs) and straight Air Gunners (AGs). As before, Tom delegated the job of getting the rest of the crew together to me.

In the Mess I got talking to a red-haired W/Op/AG who had no crew but was pleased to join us; he brought along a friend. That fixed the two W/Ops, now to find five AGs. That was solved fairly easily, as in our room was a commissioned AG. He agreed to join us and undertook to find the other four. We now had a complete crew of eleven.

The early part of the course followed the same pattern as on the Mitchell at Boundary, each crew trade working in their specialist sections until the Captains had been converted to the aeroplane. For the pilots, it was a combination of technical lectures on the systems, combined with conversion flying.

As before, we Second Pilots received just five hours conversion. The Liberator was distinct from British four-engine aeroplanes, such as the Lancaster. It was constructed to be operated by two pilots. The ignition switches, fire extinguishers and radio were located on the right sidewall of the cockpit beside the right-hand seat. The engine start switches were only just reachable from the Captain's seat, for someone with long arms. There was also a need for a third crew member to manipulate the fuel cocks, check fuel levels and monitor the generator output and switches as all of these were located behind the bulkhead aft of the Second Pilot. This was obviously the task for a Flight Engineer (FE), only at that time we did not have one and had to train the W/Ops.

During the Captain's conversion training, the instructor occupied the right-hand seat, so we Second Pilots carried out the duties of FE and attended to the Auxiliary Power Unit (APU). The APU was a two-stroke engine driving its own generator, both being located at the front of the bomb bay under the flight deck. Having the APU meant that the Liberator needed no external power supply to check systems and to start engines. The APU was always kept running on the ground to ensure that electrical power was available should the engine generators be giving too low an output due to low engine speed.

*

According to his logbook, Eric's first encounter with the Liberator was on 27th September 1944 with a two hour fifteen minute exercise as a passenger. His first at the controls, as Second Pilot, was on 28th September.

*

The Captain's conversion took a week and then it was a couple of solo sorties as a crew of five: myself, the Captain, a Navigator, a Bomb Aimer and one Wireless Operator. A dual check and further solo followed, and then it was on to night flying with an instructor aboard, and me as FE until the solo check was passed, at which point, off we went as a fivesome again. Formation came next, dual and solo for the Captain, and in the solo phase we flew with the full crew for the first time. Eleven people on board made it seem crowded until, once airborne, they all took up their crew positions, including our Ball Gunner tucked into his turret below the aeroplane.

Following the formation phase of three and six aeroplanes, we settled down to work as a crew for the navigation cross-countries. One, (the second) was carried out as a formation of three aeroplanes but the others were as a lone aeroplane. On the third, we found out how vicious the weather could be. Climbing into cloud shortly after take-off we ran into heavy icing. The airframe and propeller de-icing worked well but all our radio aerials iced up badly, drowning all signals with heavy static noise. The W/Op wound out his trailing aerial to try and get the Navigator some radio assistance, but this promptly iced up and broke off.

We had no radios and even at 25,000 feet, we were still in cloud and icing. We carried on, to complete the planned sortie and some five and a half hours later, with the Navigator having had no sight of ground or sun for a sextant shot to help him, we faced recovery with a not too accurate idea of where we were. Below us somewhere were the Rocky Mountains with heights up to 12,000 feet, so a let-down would have been a dodgy operation.

Just as the only option seemed to be to head due west, for as long as we reckoned we could safely do so and still have enough fuel to recover, I managed to identify a very weak distorted signal on the high frequency (HF) radio, from the Vancouver Radio Range.

The radio compass should have given us a bearing but, as it always did in this type of weather, it indicated the nearest thunderstorm, as it had done throughout the sortie. Using the Navigator's estimated position and the drill for finding which sector of the range we were in, a procedure that I had spent some eight hours practising on the Link at Boundary and Abbotsford, I was able to help the Captain. We finally achieved an inbound heading to the overhead and let-down, using the laid down procedure, breaking cloud fairly low, just short of what was then Sea Island airfield (now Vancouver International) and found our way back to Abbotsford, a very relieved crew. We had been airborne for seven hours and fifteen minutes, seeing the ground only on take-off and at the end of the let-down. Johnny, our Navigator, had done a splendid job under almost impossible circumstances in bringing us back just within listening range of a let-down aid.

It is worth pointing out that at that time (1944), airborne radar and very high frequency (VHF) radio was in its infancy and all we carried on the Liberator were high frequency (HF) and medium frequency (MF) radios plus the medium frequency radio compass.

Arriving back at Abbotsford there was considerable concern, as with us back, there was still one other aeroplane airborne and he would be getting short of fuel. Needless to say, no one left the Flight, just waiting for news. Eventually, due to the lapse of time it was obvious that they would not be back at Abbotsford that evening and the search of nearby units commenced, but there were no reports of them anywhere. We had to accept that they were missing. This was confirmed the next day when search aeroplanes had been sent up but with no sighting. Sadly, the crew included Maurice, the friend who had been with me since Aberystwyth, and one of the navigators with whom I had gone into Vancouver the first time and had found hospitality at Point Grey.

I was very touched that when the local radio station announced that a Liberator was missing, the Eakins family were immediately on the phone, checking that it had not been us. I was sad to have to tell them that it had been one of the navigators given hospitality next door. The aeroplane had not been found before we left Canada and I heard that it remained undiscovered until after the war, when it was found in the mountains on Vancouver Island.

This tragedy left Dave and I as the survivors of the 'Aberystwyth three', as we called ourselves, and we felt that perhaps we ought to write to Maurice's family. We knew that they would be officially notified but felt it might help if they had something from us as his friends. There was also a girlfriend in Saskatoon with whom he had been in constant contact since we had left there, and we knew she would not know what had happened. We decided that Dave should write to the family and

I would write to the girlfriend as I had met her with Maurice. This we did. Dave received a note of thanks from the family and I was asked to visit the girlfriend, as I had said that I intended to spend a few days in Saskatoon on my way back east.

Regrettably this was not the only tragedy to strike our course. The next phase was bombing training and on return from one night sortie, one crew came into the dispersal and stopped. At this two of the AGs got out of the back of the aeroplane and ran around the front to light up cigarettes, at which moment the Captain was waved forward. As he did so, the two gunners were hit and killed by the propellers Thankfully this was the last tragedy to strike during the course.

Next on the itinerary came daylight bombing, with twenty-pound practice bombs on a nearby offshore range. This involved the whole crew flying together, although in reality, only the Bomb Aimer Ray, and the Captain were fully committed. My task was to juggle the power to maintain the airspeed on the bombing run. For the gunners it was something of a bore and the Navigator just kept a watching brief.

With day bombing finished there were four more night-cross-countries and four night-bombing sorties, to finish the course. Thankfully they all passed off without any problems. Then followed the crew check, an hour-long sortie, with one of the senior instructors, during which time he threw several hypothetical emergencies at us, most of which were sorted out to his satisfaction. With that, we had finished at OTU and were declared operationally ready.

During our time at No. 5 OTU many of us had our twenty-first birthdays, myself included, so a pattern evolved of friends taking the 'Birthday Boy' out to the Hotel Vancouver for a celebration meal. Still none of us drank alcohol, so it was soft drinks, but still enjoyable.

During the party, the 'guest' would be presented with his birthday present. I was given a very nice toiletry case, which lasted many years of travel and served as a reminder of a very good group of friends, soon to be parted on posting.

Another reason for a celebration came in October when my promotion to Flying Officer came through. It had been due in August, but it took time for the necessary paperwork to be actioned.

Before the course ended, we had another surprise. Bert Heritage, one of our W/Ops, had met one of the RCAF WDs at Abbotsford. They were to be married in the church and I was asked to give the bride away. I met them in London after the war and they eventually went back to Canada, after which we lost touch.

One of the final tasks before we left Abbotsford was to dispose of the car, which was surprisingly easy. I'm sure we got the minimum for it, as the buyer knew we were leaving, but it went, and we split the proceeds. One slight problem was that Jim the Navigator of the missing aeroplane had been a part owner. However, we were able to give his share to the officer dealing with his effects, to send to his parents.

With the course completed we awaited our posting which,

when it arrived, was as expected. Back to the UK, but instead of returning through Moncton, the usual RAF route, we were to report as a crew to the RCAF depot at Lachine, just outside Montreal. We were to be there by 6th December. As it was mid-November and taking into account the five days rail travel to get there, we had fourteen days leave.

The crew disappeared to follow their own plans. I said goodbye to the Eakins family and set off for Saskatoon as I planned to say farewell to my friends there and to see Maurice's girlfriend as promised. That was a sad duty, but I hope it helped. I was surprised at how close they had been. That duty done I spent a couple of days at the home of the Reesors, my 'adoptive family'. I met some of my instructors again and finally boarded the train for Montreal. Arriving there, I spent a few days with my relatives, bought a number of presents for them and for people at home, and reported to Lachine, where the rest of the crew was gathering.

It took a few days for our draft to come through, which we 'front end crew' spent with relatives of Ray, our Bomb Aimer. They were not at all put out to have to accommodate the four of us and an enjoyable time was had by all.

On 14th December, we were all told to report back to Lachine where the whole crew was now gathered. That night, we set off by train for Halifax, Nova Scotia, en-route to the UK. Arrival at Halifax in the early morning gave us our first sight of our transport home. It was the Cunard liner RMS Mauritania alongside the quay.

CHAPTER 10

RETURN ATLANTIC CROSSING

Once on board we found that, as officers, we would not be on troop decks, as on our outward voyage eighteen months previously. In fact, we were accommodated in what, in peacetime, had been a first-class suite; the snag was that sixteen of us were crammed into it! The plus side, however, was that we would have our meals in the ship's dining room, with ship stewards waiting on our table and food cooked by the ship's catering staff. The voyage home was much as the voyage out had been, with little to do but watch the sea go by, bet on the ship's daily mileage and chat.

There was the usual lifeboat drill on leaving harbour and again we were unescorted. At this time the U-boat threat had vastly decreased but lifebelts were still our constant companions. I was very pleased to meet my instructor from Bowden, Sgt. Webb on deck one evening. He had completed his tour as an instructor and hoped to be going to a fighter squadron when home. I wonder if he did; I never met him again.

As the voyage progressed, excitement grew as Christmas was approaching. Would we make home in time? On Christmas Eve, we had a Christmas dinner with all the trimmings, laid on by the caterers and were told that we were in the approaches to Liverpool where we would dock the next morning. The next morning came and there were the famous Liver Birds as we docked.

Off the ship and onto a train, it came as an eye-opener to see the damage and dilapidation of England again after the bright lights and prosperity of Canada, but we were home. I did not finally arrive home until Boxing Day, having spent Christmas night on the train south to London. I then had until 12th January at home, before reporting to No. 9 Personnel Reception Centre (PRC) in the spa town of Harrogate in Yorkshire.

Once settled at home, the leave followed much the same pattern as before I went to Canada. The first place to visit was my old school, for it was here that we were usually able to catch up on the whereabouts of friends. This time however, it was a sad visit as I found that my closest school friend, Alan Taylor, had been killed in France and that five of the school rugby team, in which I had played in my last year, had also been killed. There were other old boys of whom I had heard but they had been ahead of me in the school.

During the leave, I visited Alan's parents. I had spent many weekends with them, during my last year at school and in the two years following, before Alan had joined the army and I the RAF. It was a very sad visit, but they made me welcome; they were doing their best to hide their grief.

It was also during this leave that I heard that one of my cousins from Yorkshire had also been killed in France. It was not a happy leave, although it was good to be home with my parents. My father was very busy as he had been made overall head gardener for several local estates that had been taken over by the War Department for food production. He spent much time cycling around the area visiting them. Additionally, he was an Air Raid Warden but luckily that did not take up too many of his nights, as raids were infrequent. This was at the time of the V1 and V2 attacks, so there were alerts.

My mother, as with so many housewives in Britain at that time, was doing her best at coping with the meagre rations, but because they were out in the country and she had local garden produce available, was not having quite the struggle that some people in the towns were having. It was still obviously taking its toll, as she looked much older than when I had gone to Canada.

On 12th January 1945 I duly reported to Harrogate, to find the PRC located in one of the large hotels. The next four days were mainly occupied by various administration tasks and form filling. Most forms seemed to require a full crew list so that crews could be posted together. With ten names to go on each form, this became somewhat tedious.

Since the unit also handled aircrew who had returned directly from training bases in Canada and the USA, they had to be properly kitted up for Europe, so were issued with clothing coupons, as were we. I spent most of the four days arguing that as I had bought my uniforms in Canada, I should not forfeit clothing coupons, as did those who had to purchase uniforms in Harrogate. I finally won, so my mother got them.

For ourselves it was confirmed what we had expected, that we would be going out to India to join a squadron there. We were given the opportunity to buy tropical kit, but the general advice was to take the minimum UK style kit and to buy the rest in India, as the tailoring there was much better and more stylish. This we did.

INDIA

&

BURMA

JAN 1945 - OCT 1946

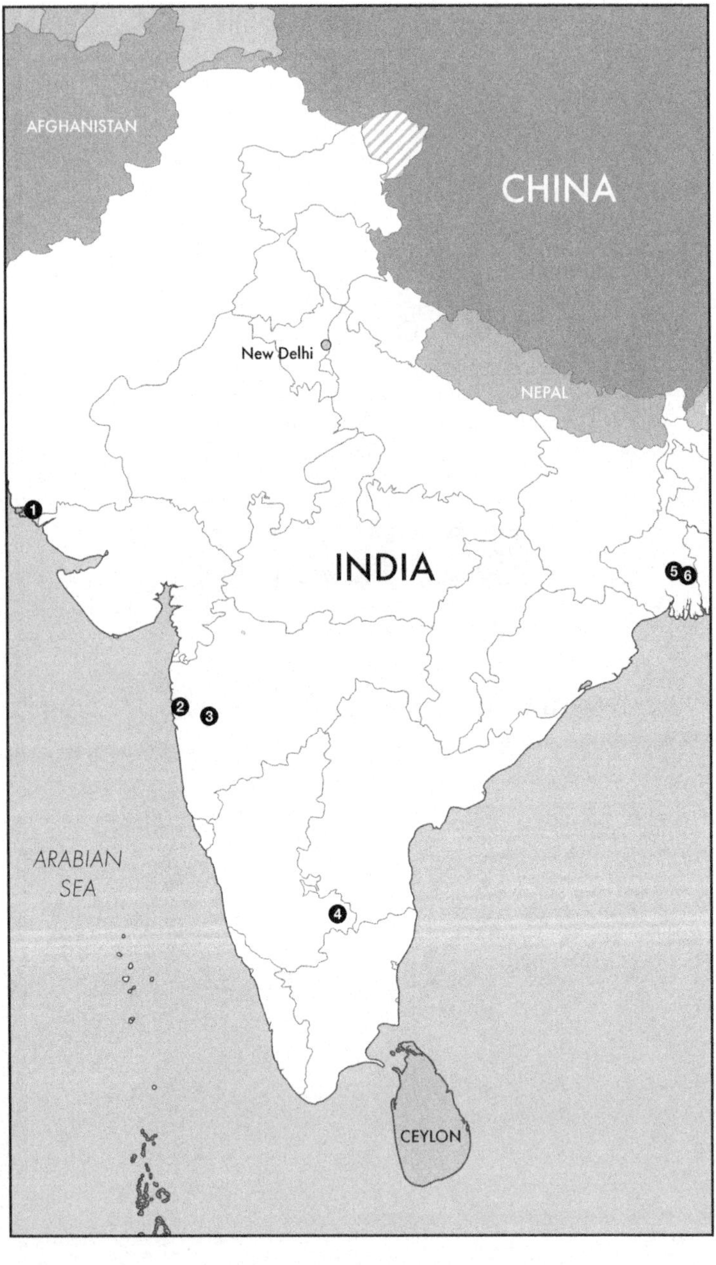
AFGHANISTAN
CHINA
New Delhi
NEPAL
INDIA
1
2
3
4
5
6
ARABIAN
SEA
CEYLON

JAN 1945 - OCT 1946

1. KARACHI

2. BOMBAY (NOW MUMBAI)

3. POONA (NOW PUNE)*

4. KOLAR*

5. DIGRI*

6. CALCUTTA (NOW KOLKATA)

7. PEGU (NOW BAGO)*

8. MYITKYINA*

* STATIONS AT WHICH ERIC SERVED

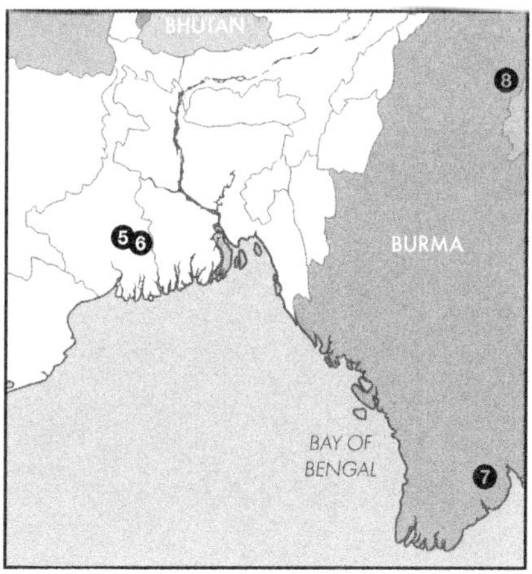

CHAPTER 11

TRAVEL TO INDIA

To our surprise, once our posting was confirmed, we were told that we were priority reinforcements and would be flown out to India by the quickest means possible. To meet this requirement, we were posted immediately to No. 18 Personnel Despatch Centre (PDC) in London, where we arrived on 16th January 1945 to find that again, we were in a large block of flats near Lord's Cricket Ground. I had gone full circle.

Once settled in, we had to report as a crew to the RAF Liaison Officer at the BOAC terminal at Victoria, where we learned that we would be flown out by BOAC Sunderland aeroplane from Poole in two days' time. This gave us a couple of days in London, at that time the target of the V2 rockets, to take in the atmosphere of the capital and to dance again (ballroom) at Covent Garden Opera House.

We were off next to Poole and the BOAC Flying Boat base where we were accommodated in a hotel as BOAC passengers.

Unfortunately, our move coincided with a spell of extremely cold, bad weather that prevented flying, so we did not get airborne until 29th January. On the morning of the 29th, Sunderland ML 751 lumbered into the air from Poole harbour (a water take-off being a new experience) and climbed to the south to cross western France, bound for Djerba in North Africa.

The aeroplane crew consisted of an RAF Squadron Leader and Flight Lieutenant and as well as the eleven of us, there were four civilians on board. There were no cabin staff but there was food in the galley and hot drinks in thermos flasks. We took it in turns to act as stewards, looking after the civilians. As the aeroplane climbed over France to have enough altitude to clear the high ground in southern France, it was evident that the heating system had frozen up. It became bitterly cold and there were only two thin blankets provided at each seat; then someone had a bright idea. Our kit was in the hold and in it was our cold weather flying gear; the kitbags were opened and full flying gear plus fur-lined boots donned. That meant that we could pile all our blankets on the shivering civilians. In this way we, and they, survived the eight-and-a-half-hour leg.

The accommodation at Djerba was under canvas but in rather plush tents and it was beautifully warm. After a meal and a stroll around the small village nearby, it was off to have a comfortable night's sleep.

After breakfast the next morning, it was out to the aeroplane in a passenger tender. We scrambled aboard hoping not to fall in the water – no one did and so we took off for Cairo. This was a much more pleasant leg. It was warm as we flew along the north African coast, passing over the land that had been so heavily fought over some two years previously, to land on the River Nile at Cairo.

Leaving the aeroplane and safely on dry land, we were whisked off in a BOAC bus to spend the night in Shepherds Hotel. It was nice to travel with VIPs, as our civilians obviously were. The leg from Djerba to Cairo took just over seven hours and gave us a chance to climb the ladder to the flight deck and investigate the sharp end which was very different to the Liberator.

After the night stop, we were airborne fairly early for the short leg across the desert, to a re-fuelling stop at Habbaniyah in Iraq. This was reached in four and a half hours and we landed on a lake. With re-fuelling completed, passengers were back aboard after light refreshments ashore and we were then airborne on another short leg to Bahrein (known as Bahrain since the 1950s), another four and a half hours away. Bahrein was much warmer than Cairo, but we passed a comfortable night there in a hotel. The following morning, we were airborne early on the last leg of the flight; our destination was Karachi in what is now Pakistan.

At the end of this six hour thirty minute flight, we landed on the flying boat terminus there and said goodbye to our VIP civilians. They expressed their thanks for our attention during the flight, wished us luck and to give the Japanese hell, then went off in High Commission cars while we were picked up by an RAF truck and taken to a large transit camp where we spent the next three weeks getting bored and playing endless games of Monopoly.

It did give us time to get rid of our cold weather flying gear and to get ourselves kitted out in tropical kit tailored by the camp tailor and as we had been told, it was much superior to that issued in the UK, and it didn't need clothing coupons. During this wait at Karachi, we were joined by another crew from our course at Abbotsford. It was the crew in which my friend Dave, the other member of the Aberystwyth duo, was Second Pilot. From this time on until I left India in August 1946, his crew and mine remained together even when he and I later became Captains.

Finally came the time to leave for the Refresher Flying Unit (RFU) at Kolar in Central India. That meant a three-day journey by Indian Railways, first across the Sindh desert, then via Ahmedabad and Hyderabad to Bangalore, where we detrained and went by road to Kolar.

The train journey was an experience easily forgotten. We officers shared double berth compartments sleeping on the two bunks but, when we found our NCOs were condemned to third-class carriages with slatted seats, we crammed them into our compartments. Needless to say, there was no such thing as air conditioning and a small ceiling fan was all there was to churn the very hot air around.

The RFU was exactly what its name suggested and for the two weeks there, once the Captain had been checked out night and day, we flew as a crew covering local flying, cross-countries (day and night) and bombing with practice 20lb bombs (day and night), plus some formation and most exciting, fighter affiliation, where we were subject to attacks by Hurricane fighters from nearby Bangalore. That kept the gunners busy and showed what an excellent fighter the Hurricane was. It also indicated to us that the odds were on the fighter if well flown, despite our ten Browning .50 calibre guns.

Now it was time to find which of the seven Liberator squadrons we would go to. It turned out to be 159 Squadron at Digri, up north, some sixty miles west of Calcutta. Again, we were faced with a long (four day) train journey, which followed the same pattern as that from Karachi, with our NCOs again sharing our compartments. The journey took us up the east coast of India to Kharagpur, where we detrained and found the inevitable truck to take us to Digri. It was 27th March 1945.[4]

Eric captioned this 'nice hat'!

4 See *Historical Context* section, page 223, for more informaton.

CHAPTER 12

159 SQUADRON

Digri turned out to be built to what was a standard pattern for RAF Stations of that time. As at Kolar, the accommodation was in 'bashas'. These were huts built on concrete bases with sides and roofs made of woven bamboo leaves, with a gap between the wall and roof to allow air to circulate. Inside the officers' basha, shared by two officers (junior), there were two 'charpoys' - wooden framed beds. The frames were interwoven with coarse cord, on which we slept, using our camp kit that had been issued at Karachi.

There was provision to hang our mosquito nets, which were essential. However, for a reason we found out later, mosquitoes were not as bad a torment as might have been expected given our location. During the day, the net was tied back and it was dropped as evening approached. We each had a wardrobe and there was a table between the beds. There was room beside the beds to stand the canvas washbasin, which was part of the camp kit.

Two of us shared the services of a 'bearer'. He wore the same uniform as the Mess staff but it was our responsibility to pay him a set rate each month and to tip him for extra services. Behind the basha there was a concrete platform where the bearer would set out our camp baths each evening. These were three-feet long, square canvas affairs, supported by a collapsible frame. Upon filling it with hot water, he would proclaim 'bath ready Sahib'. We then took our open-air baths.

By comparison with the 14th Army in the jungles of Burma, our accommodation was palatial and civilised but we were still subject to the attentions of malarial mosquitoes, and the heat and high humidity of Bengal, which soon resulted in the appearance of prickly heat, a rash all over the body due to constant sweating, day and night. With the arrival of the monsoon, many of us found that the rash turned septic and was extremely painful. The standard treatment to alleviate the condition was to cover it with a cream called Gentian Violet so, soon many of us were going around sprouting purple patches, not always where they were visible, as the condition struck most in areas of the body subject to local body heat.

The Officers' Mess was of similar construction to the bashas but was obviously larger and contained a kitchen, dining room, anteroom and a bar. The Mess staff were all Indian and were very good at their job. They wore white uniforms with a red/blue headband. Many had been in the employment of the Service for some years.

We decided that the Captain (Tom) and I should share a

room. The Navigator and Bomb Aimer, Johnny and Ray would share and our Officer A/G Don, would share with an A/G from the other new crew. Settled into our basha, we went across to the Mess to have a meal, to meet other officers and to find out about the squadron.

We found that we had been lucky in our posting. Of the seven Liberator[5] squadrons in the Group (231), four operated in the formation bombing role just as the Americans did in Europe, two were 'Special Duties', involved with clandestine operations behind Japanese lines with the guerrilla forces of Force 136 and the last, 159 (ours) operated mostly independently, carrying out mining and interdiction strikes on rail transport and bridges, with occasional conventional bombing sorties but not in formation.

We also learned that the previous CO, Wing Commander Blackburn had, by reducing crew numbers, taking out armour plates, the ball turret and the waist guns, made the aeroplane lighter, thus significantly increasing the bomb load from 3,000 pounds, for the conventional Liberator, to 8,000 pounds. In October and December 1944, he had taken fifteen aeroplanes of the squadron on a mining sortie to Penang, a round trip of over 3,000 miles, lasting over twenty-one hours. At that time, it was the longest armed sortie of the war and had confounded the American Liberator squadrons in the theatre. We had obviously joined a top line unit with high morale.

All of this was confirmed by the incumbent CO, Wing

5 See *Historical Context* section, page 229, for more informaton.

Commander Ercolani (of post-war Ercol furniture fame), when we met him the next morning.

Having met the CO, we went along to the squadron Flight offices to meet our Flight Commander Tommy Watson, an RCAF Flight Lieutenant.

He introduced us to some of the other crews there and we found that at least half of the squadron was Canadian. Unfortunately, we then found that 159 flew with reduced crews all the time, a legacy of the previous CO, so we would have to drop one W/Op and three A/Gs but would gain a Flight Engineer. It was difficult to make these choices, but it had to be done.

The Captain, Tom, discussed it with me and eventually we decided to keep the tail gunner, and move our commissioned gunner from the waist position into the front turret. This meant that we lost the front, ball and one waist gunner and on balance, we decided to keep the W/Op, Bert, who had got married just before we left OTU. In action, the mid-upper turret would be manned by the W/Op. The surplus crew was posted to other squadrons in the Group.

We also found out the reason why the mosquitoes were not as bad as might have been expected. On the opposite side of the airfield was a Flight of three black-painted Liberators. They were manned by crews who had completed a tour of operations and were now on operational 'rest'. Their task was to fly over the front lines in Burma at night, spraying the areas with insecticide (DDT), which they carried in their bomb bay tanks, after which the ground troops got some relief from the mosquitoes. It often happened that they returned with some DDT still on board, so they sprayed the camp before landing, hence less mosquitoes at Digri. The Flight had an official number but was universally known as 'Flit Flight'. Some operational 'rest'!

Having settled into the squadron we then flew an intensive series of day and night bombing sorties, mostly at medium level, but with an introduction to low level (fifty feet) thrown in. That made us ready for operations.

During the training sorties the Captain had been 'blooded' by flying as Second Pilot on an operation with an experienced crew. So, on 18th April 1945 we were briefed for our first war operation which was to lay 6,000 pounds of mines off Heinze Bay, south of Akyab, on the Burmese coast. The drop was successful; there was no opposition and the trip took twelve and three-quarter hours.

By comparison with Europe, there was only light opposition in the theatre. At this time, the 14th Army was in control of northern Burma and was moving south towards Rangoon, so the Japanese fighters had been pulled back and generally only appeared over the front lines at the major targets such as Rangoon and Bangkok, at ports and railway choke points.

Similarly, the anti-aircraft (A/A) opposition was generally met over such targets. However, it was not the enemy alone that formed the hazards to our operations.

First, the distance of 2,000 (plus) miles was a normal sortie; next came the terrain. No one walked back after crashing in

159 Sqn. Digri, Eric with Ray, Bomb Aimer.

159 Sqn. VE day at Digri - Drumhead Service.

War operation No. 4. Bombing bridges at Ban Tak Kam.

War operation No. 4. Bombing bridges at Ban Tak Kam.

the jungle and no crews who went into the Bay of Bengal were rescued. That just left the weather. During the monsoon, the clouds could build up to above 30,000 feet and the conditions inside them could, and did, break up aeroplanes. We hit one storm just off the Ganges delta as we returned one night. We had no warning as we had been in cloud for some time. Suddenly the aeroplane, all 50,000 pounds of it, was hit by terrific turbulence, with high climb rates followed by huge descent rates. The vibrations were so violent that we could not read the instruments and with both of us on the controls, were struggling to maintain some semblance of control. Then, just as suddenly the turbulence ceased and we were out into the clear moonlight. Luckily there was no obvious damage and the crew, although badly shaken, had been able to find handholds so there were no injuries.

Back at base, the next day saw more bombing practice just to keep us on our toes. Two days later we were detailed for our second operation the following day and duly got out of bed early for breakfast to be followed by briefing. At this point I was hit by amoebic dysentery and ended up in the Mobile Field Hospital, co-located at Digri.

Despite treatment with the new sulpha drugs, my stay lasted for ten days so I missed several operations including the invasion and occupation of Rangoon where the squadron took part in bombing the A/A positions.

Back with the crew again, we took part in two more mining operations, the squadron's speciality, involving one flight of thirteen hours, thirty minutes and the other of fourteen hours, both in excess of 2,500 miles. On the return flight from the first of these, after midnight on 7th May, the W/Op, who often tuned into the radio news, came on the intercom and said: 'It's ok chaps, the war is over!' He had heard that 8th May was to be Victory in Europe (VE) Day. We cheered and the next day went off on our third operation.

Operation No. 4 was a low level bombing attack on a bridge on the infamous Burma Railway. It was successful; we flew for 2,680 miles, but we had to divert and land at Akyab as we were short of fuel after eleven hours flying.

Operation No. 5 brought our first taste of heavy and light A/A fire as the target was a submarine depot ship at Sattahip Bay in Siam (now Thailand). We were tasked to suppress the A/A fire with four others, whilst the rest of the squadron went in at low level and sank the ship; this was 2,250 miles and fourteen hours thirty minutes flying. The bomb load for this operation comprised forty pound anti-personnel bombs, held together by wire slings in clusters of five on the bomb hooks. With twenty clusters in the bomb bay, this gave the Bomb Aimer quite a task to remove the safety pins before we took off. Despite the A/A fire, which was quite heavy until we and the others intervened, there were no casualties to the low-level attack force.

That saw us to the end of May and into June, with another mining operation to the Bay of Bandon; that was 2,670 miles and fourteen hours and forty-five minutes.

With the Japanese almost out of Burma, targets were not

as plentiful as they had been, and we only flew one more operation in June. That was an A/A suppression trip to a bridge at Kanchanaburi with two of the other group squadrons (355 and 356) bombing in formation from medium level. There were in fact two bridges, a steel one and a wooden by-pass that had been built by Allied prisoners of war from a nearby camp.

The bridges were destroyed; the sortie lasted fourteen hours and the round trip was 2,410 miles. On this target, we received a much more hostile reception but there were no casualties in the attacking force, so our efforts must have been effective. Hostilities certainly decreased markedly as the raid progressed. We claimed a hit on a heavy A/A site. On this target, the 'Master Bomber' technique was used for the first time by the 'Forgotten Air Force', one of our Flight Commanders performing the task, and relaying target information to us of the A/A sites to be taken out. We Second Pilots were briefed to listen for his instructions over the HF radio sets. We still had no VHF radios, unlike UK Bomber Command. These sets eventually arrived with the introduction of the Liberator Mk. VIII.

The river that the bridges crossed was the River Kwai. Many years later, a very successful film was made about these bridges, but it used a lot of artistic licence in its portrayal.

At this time the squadron was receiving new Mark VIII Liberators to replace our Mark VIs. They had a completely different internal layout, as for the first time we had a Mark XIII radar fitted. This brought the Navigator and Bomb Aimer from the nose compartment up to the rear of the flight deck, in front of the mid-upper turret and put the W/Op in the centre of the aeroplane above the bomb bay. The Pilot's side windows were bowed instead of flat and this considerably improved vision. Additionally, the aileron controls, which on the earlier Liberators had been heavy, were given servo assistance.

A new experience followed. With the Japanese almost out of Burma we, as a crew, were detached to Jessore (now Jashore, Bangledesh), to the northeast of Digri, to join 357 and 358 Squadrons there to drop supplies to Force 136 operating behind the Japanese lines. After a practice drop on the airfield, we were off on Operation No. 8 but developed a bad hydraulic leak and had to abort. With the aeroplane repaired, we repeated the briefed sortie the next day. This time it was successful at 2,347 miles and twelve hours fifty-five minutes.

Operation No. 10 on 3rd August was also a supply drop to Force 136. This was quite a short trip at nine hours and 2,028 miles.

We then returned to Digri where I requested a change of crew. There had been growing friction between Tom and I over the fact that whereas some of the other Second Pilots were sharing the flying with their Captains, including take-offs and landings, that had not been the case with us. I only ever flew the aeroplane when out over the sea and only on return from operations.

My request was granted, and I crewed up with another Captain who had been a Second Pilot but was now converting to Captain. Co-incident with this of course was the dropping

War operation No. 7. Bridges at Kanchanaburi destroyed.

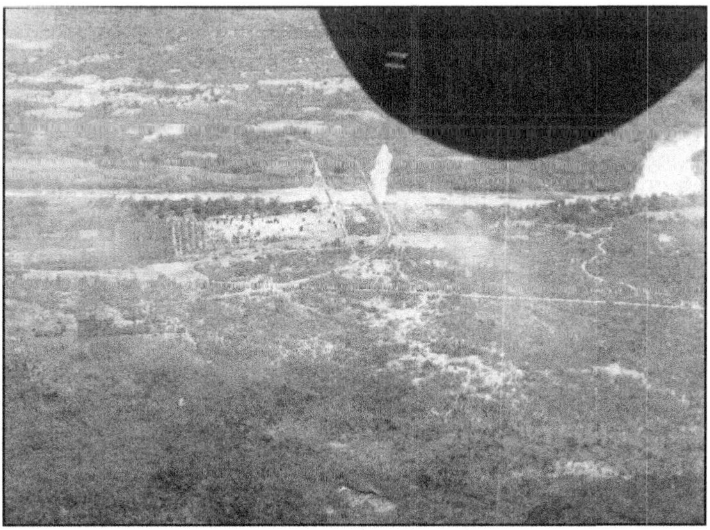

War operation No. 7. Bridges at Kanchanaburi destroyed.

of the atomic bombs on Japan, who sued for peace. The new Captain and I carried on with his conversion and the CO made the decision that my friend Dave and I should also start conversion to First Pilot and, when aeroplanes were available, to Captain.

First, of course, came the celebration of Victory Over Japan (VJ) Day on 15th August 1945. The squadron stood down for two days, a Drumhead Service was held with the whole Station on parade and then the various Messes celebrated in their own way.

On my twenty-second birthday on 17th August, we started work again continuing the conversions but in September, the squadron was tasked with supply dropping in what was then French Indo-China (now Vietnam). I did three supply drops at Saigon. These trips were shorter than would have been the case from India because we were now able to stage through Pegu in Burma. They averaged between nine and ten hours and were 1,700 miles. The last one was an exception as we staged Pegu-Saigon-Digri, which took twelve hours forty-five minutes and 2,620 miles.

We then switched our efforts to Ubon, working from the Jessore base, a sortie of fourteen hours and fifty-five minutes and 2,720 miles. For some reason, Group ruled that these sorties counted as war operations and were so logged; that brought my total operations up to sixteen.

The final operation, No. 17, was a supply drop at a Force 136 camp but we received the wrong recognition signals and aborted. That flight took thirteen hours and all for no result.

That completed my war operational flying. I believe that we were allowed to log the last flights over Indo-China as war operations because many of the Japanese forces there had not surrendered and were still fighting. The date was 3rd November 1945.

*

Eric remained with 159 Squadron at Digri completing his conversion to Captain, including trips to Bombay, Lahore and Karachi. On 29th January 1946, his logbook was annotated by the Squadron Commander:

> *'CERTIFIED THAT 163834 F/O*
> *MARKWELL E. IS QUALIFIED TO*
> *CAPTAIN LIBERATOR AIRCRAFT W.E.F.*
> *29.1.46*
> *WING COMMANDER, COMMANDING 159*
> *SQDN RAF'*

Following his conversion to Captain, Eric flew thirty-three sorties (often three a day), rice dropping for humanitarian support during February 1946. Interestingly a new type sneaks into Eric's logbook on 24th February - a Lancaster listed as 'A310' and flown as Second Pilot on a local one hour five minute sortie. I can only surmise that this was a visiting aeroplane and Eric took the opportunity to try it out and compare it to the Liberator.

Rice dropping continued in March and April with thirty sorties but switched from Pegu to Myitkyina, operating alongside 355 Squadron. The trips to Myitkyina were around six hours which allowed for only one trip, per aeroplane, per day. Bomb bay panniers were fitted which increased the load from eighty-eight to ninety-four bags, weighing in at 7,520 pounds.

A 159 Sqn. Liberator Mk. VIII.

Eric's Liberator crew at 159 Squadron.
Back row: Arthur, Jonah, Jock R, Jock G. Front row: Eric, Jack and Ken.

MYITKYINA SOUTH

GENERAL INFORMATION

1. OBSTRUCTIONS
   SURROUNDED BY HILLS UP TO 2000FT.,
   5-10 MILES.
2. AIRFIELD LIGHTING
   ELECTRIC FLAREPATH ON REQUEST.
3. SERVICING
   AVAILABLE.
4. ACCOMMODATION
   AVAILABLE.
5. SPECIAL INFORMATION
   RUNWAY: ALL WEATHER
   SUITABLE FOR ALL TYPES.

RADIO AIDS

(1) Radar Beacon — NO
(2) M/F. D/F. — NO
(3) H/F. D/F. — YES
(4) Beam Approach — NIL
(5) M/F Beacon. — YES
Characteristic — FC
(6) V.H.F. D/F. — YES
Callsign — FC
(7) Airfield Control
Tower Transmits — 206 Kcs. 116.1 Mcs.
Receives — 4496 Kcs. 116.1 Mcs.
Call Sign — FC

Airfield plate for Myitkyina from Eric's logbook.

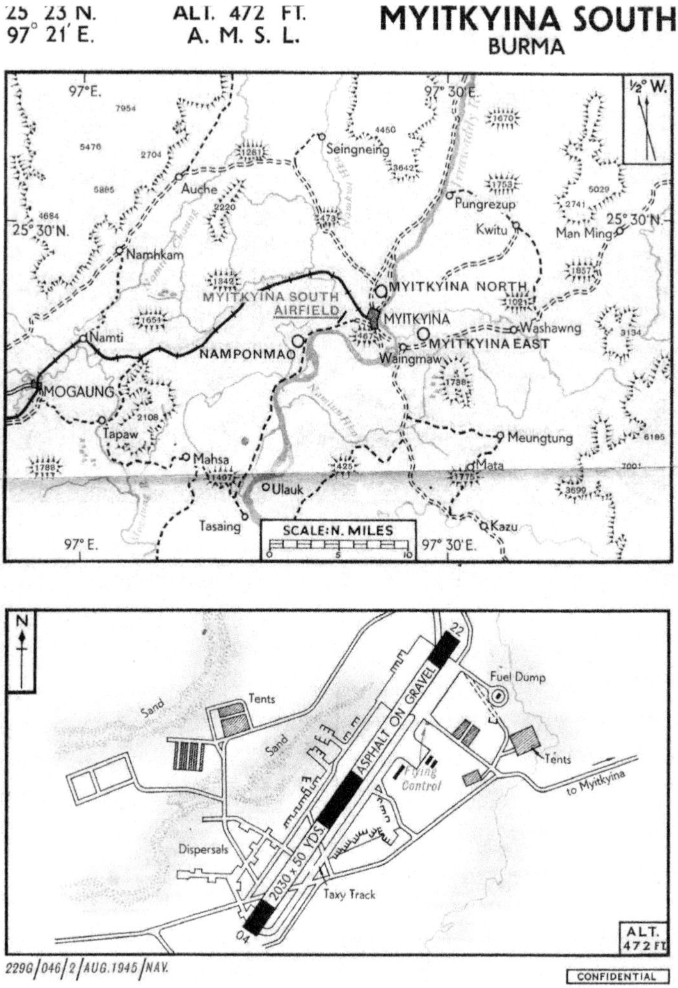

Airfield plate for Myitkyina from Eric's logbook.

UNITED KINGDOM

NOV 1946 - AUG 1956

NOV 1946 - AUG 1956

1. BURTONWOOD
2. CHALGROVE
3. LEUCHARS*
4. KIRKHAM
5. WOODLEY*
6. MORETON-IN-MARSH*
7. SOUTH CERNEY*
8. LITTLE RISSINGTON*
9. CRANWELL*

* STATIONS AT WHICH ERIC SERVED

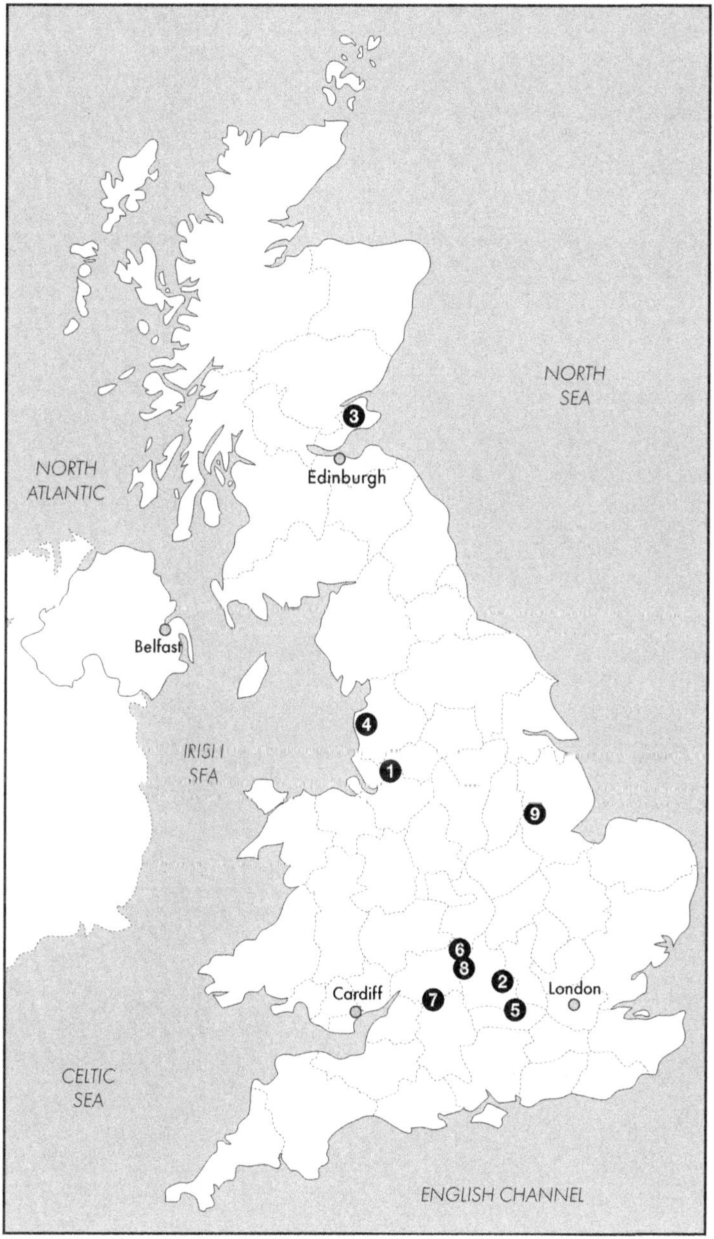
NORTH SEA
NORTH ATLANTIC
Edinburgh
Belfast
IRISH SEA
Cardiff
London
CELTIC SEA
ENGLISH CHANNEL
1
2
3
4
5
6
7
8
9

CHAPTER 13

FINAL DAYS OF SERVICE AND RETURN TO ENGLAND

In mid May 1946, 159 Squadron was disbanded and many of its crews, including Eric, transferred to 232 Squadron at Poona (now Pune). His logbook shows that his last trip with 159 was on 9th May 1945, with a total of fifteen hours for the month.

In the meantime, his promotion to Flight Lieutenant (back-dated to 11th February) had come through. Eric flew a further seventy-nine hours with 232 Squadron, including a three-hour conversion to the C87, the transport version of the Liberator, making his last Liberator flight, an air test on 16th July 1946.

Eric left 232 Squadron on 28th August 1946. Travelling to Bombay, he embarked on the SS Georgic for the return journey to England on 1st September, arriving on 19th and transferring to No. 5 PDC at Burtonwood.

From Burtonwood he moved initially to 21 Aircrew Holding Unit (ACHU) Chalgrove on 21st October and as an instructor to No. 3 General Reconnaissance School (GRS) at Leuchars on 8th November.

At Leuchars, Eric found himself re-united with the Anson, this time the aging Mk. I. His first trip was on 21st November 1946, his first training session for students being 3rd December.

Eric continued with flying training until being demobilised in April 1947, making his last trip in Anson (R) on 18th April. Ironically this entry, together with the various summaries, closed his first logbook on 23rd April 1947. Eric left the RAF with 1,017 hours 35 minutes total time, and an above average assessment as a pilot.

Eric left Leuchars on 27th April for No. 101 Personnel Despatch Centre (PDC), Kirkham, being released on 28th April, with his last day of service recorded as 1st August 1947. He returned to Barclays Bank in Haslemere.

On 11th March 1948, Eric married Georgie (the lady mentioned earlier) at St. Christopher's Church Haslemere, Surrey. In June 1950, Eric joined the RAFVR, attending a fifteen-day annual training course at Woodley, flying just under thirty hours on Tiger Moths.

Banking clearly did not suit him, and on 12th June 1951 Eric re-joined the RAF at Hendon on an eight-year short service commission, moving immediately to Central Flying School (CFS) detachment at Moreton-in-Marsh. Here he converted to the Harvard, first encountered in Canada,

Mr & Mrs Markwell.
St. Christopher's Church, Haslemere, Surrey. 11th March 1948.

CFS 'E' Flight.
Eric (centre) with colleagues.

CFS 'E' Flight Cranwell, sometime post June 1952.
Eric is front row centre. The aircraft is a Boulton Paul Balliol.

CFS 'E' Flight.
Eric is front row, 3rd from left.

'Tiger bashing' at Woodley.

Eric, Tiger bashing at Woodley.

Harvards up from Little Rissington.

RAF Brüggen main gate.

Meteor WL413 was one of several Eric flew at Brüggen.

followed by detachments on 25th July to South Cerney and on 1st October to Little Rissington.

During this period, Eric also converted to the Percival Prentice and soloed on the Meteor T7, qualifying as Qualified Flying Instructor (QFI). On 19th November, Eric moved again to Cranwell, commencing his career as an instructor on the Harvard. It had been quite a year.

Eric remained at Cranwell until the beginning of August 1954, adding over 700 hours teaching, and converting to the Chipmunk, Vampire, Balliol and Anson XXI. He had received promotion to Flight Lieutenant on 19th June 1952 (having re-joined as a Flying Officer) and became a CFS Flight Commander on 28th April 1954.

In August 1954 Eric was posted back to South Cerney as a QFI, where he converted to the Piston Provost, spent some time on the Auster 7 and was introduced to jets with the Vampire T11.

In February 1955, he had a familiarisation session on the Firefly T7. May saw further Meteor T7 time and in August 1955 he had his first session and soloed in the Jet Provost.

1956 saw further Provost and Meteor time and an introduction to the Hunter F4 with five sorties in February. Whilst not classed as supersonic, the Hunter would go supersonic in a dive. Eric recorded two such milestones in these five sorties. On 14th August, with 2,741 hours, 35 minutes flying time in his logbook, Eric was posted to RAF Brüggen in

Germany and moved there with his family.[6]

This was technically a ground posting as Station Intelligence Officer (SIO) but Eric kept flying with No. 135 Wing, mostly in Vampire T11s but also the Prentice.

Through 1957, in spite of his Intelligence Officer duties, Eric added twenty-eight hours in the Vampire, nine hours thirty minutes in the Chipmunk, nine hours fifteen minutes in the Meteor and one hour thirty minutes in the Canberra T4.

A side duty occurred on 11th March 1957 when HRH Prince Philip paid a visit to Brüggen, Eric was appointed Official Photographer (note the arm band in the photo).

Through to November 1958, Eric added a further eleven hours and forty minutes in the Meteor and five hours and forty minutes of Chipmunk time. Whilst Eric had 'kept his hand in', as we know from his return to the RAF from the bank, desks were not for him.

Here he describes what happened next…

6 See *Historical Context* section, page 231, for more informaton.

Eric Markwell, Royal Photographer!

HRH Prince Philip arriving at RAF Brüggen, 11th March 1957.

HRH. climbing onto Javelin XA 566 of 87 Squadron.

HRH (front) inspects Javelin XA 566 of 87 Squadron.

GERMANY

AUG 1956 - JULY 1961

AUG 1956 - JULY 1961

1. LANDSBERG / PENZING*

2. BRÜGGEN*

3. AHLHORN

4. MEMMINGEN*

5. MENGEN*

6. KAUFBEUREN*

* STATIONS AT WHICH ERIC SERVED

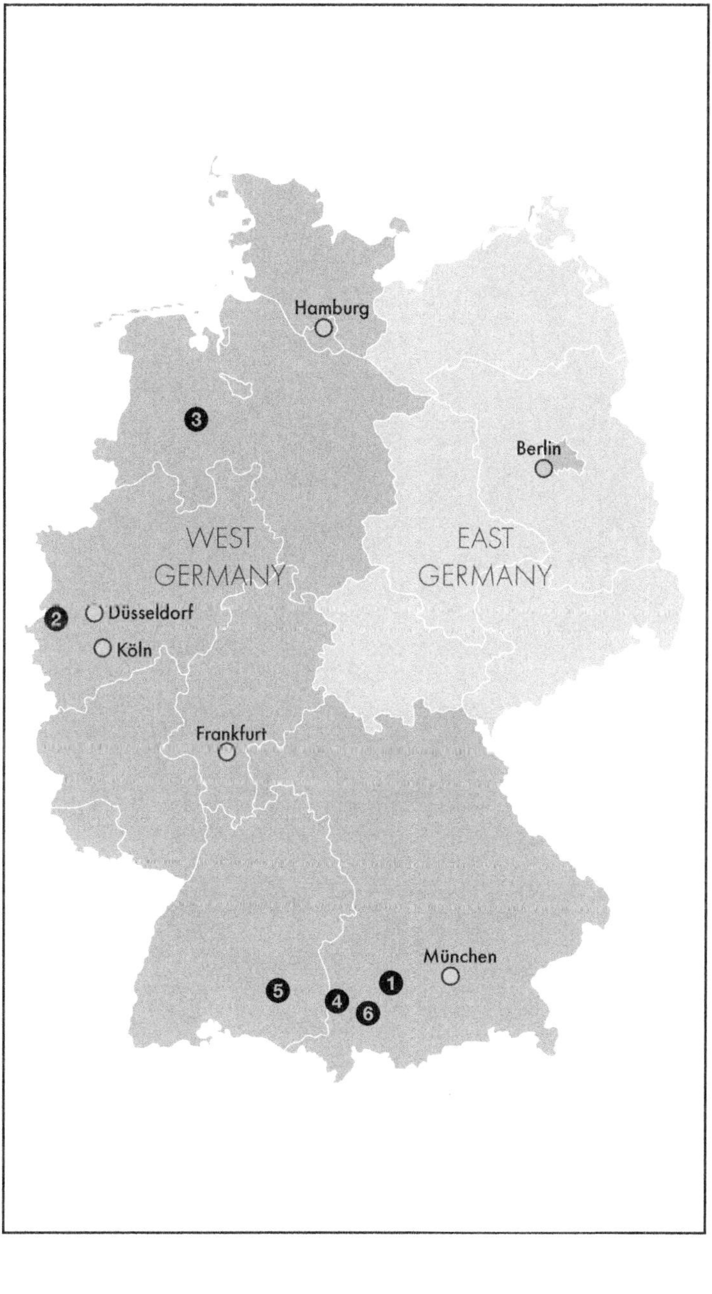
Hamburg
3
Berlin
WEST
GERMANY
EAST
GERMANY
2
Düsseldorf
Köln
Frankfurt
München
1
5
4
6

CHAPTER 14

RAF MISSION TO THE GERMAN AIR FORCE

In the autumn of 1958, the Air Ministry (not then the MOD) issued a circular advising that the RAF had undertaken a commitment to assist the German Air Force (GAF - it reverted to the Luftwaffe later), with pilot training. The unit would be called the 'RAF Mission to the German Air Force' and would be based at Landsberg in Bavaria where it would integrate with the GAF training school there.

To staff the unit, planned at fifty Qualified Flying Instructors (QFIs), interested QFIs were to submit posting applications through the usual channels. No stipulation was made of the need to speak German and I found that few of the 'Missionaries' were fluent in the language. I was just approaching the end of my tour as the SIO at RAF Brüggen, a ground posting. The chance of a return to flying, combined with another tour in Germany (particularly Bavaria) was tempting, so I submitted my application.

In due course I was notified that I had been successful and a posting notice arrived. However, since I had been on a ground tour I was detached to RAF Manby in December for a refresher flying course on the Piston Provost. On arrival at Manby I found that my instructor there would be an officer who had been one of my students when I had been a staff QFI on the CFS Waterfront flying the Provost - it's a small world! Also on the course were two others posted to the Mission.

Completion of the course, plus travelling time to and from the UK took care of the month of December, so I returned to Brüggen for Christmas 1958.

Early in January 1959, I reported to Landsberg to find that I was one of the last of the RAF instructors to arrive and the Mission was in being. There was a small headquarters under the command of a Wing Commander, a Squadron Leader Flying and an Adjutant, with a small number of administrative staff.

Many of the early arrivals had already been joined by their families and were living in the flats that had been converted for us from barrack blocks at the Landsberg Kaserne (military barracks). There was also a junior school for our young children. Medical cover would be provided by the Station Medical Officer, a GAF Flight Surgeon, with hospital cover if needed at the US forces hospital in Augsburg.

When my family joined me, we moved in to one of the flats

in the Kaserne. The flat was well furnished to RAF standards but lacked sound-proofing and extraneous noise could be a problem. The German Army operated the Walker Bulldog tank, a number of which were stationed at the Kaserne and used to depart 0600 with all the noise you would expect.

Of the fifty QFIs, half had been posted to Ahlhorn in north Germany, to carry out basic instruction there, on (I think) a Piaggio aeroplane, whilst the rest would be remaining at Landsberg to complete the student training on the Harvard.

Next came something of a cultural shock. It seemed that when the GAF had reformed after the Second World War, the initial setting-up and training of the cadre of the force was carried out by the United States Air Force (USAF) and so they adopted the USAF system and nomenclature themselves. So instead of being allocated a room in the Officers' Mess, I found myself in a BOQ (Bachelor Officers' Quarter) and the Mess was the Officers' Club.

A further shock was to follow, as I was told that I would have to do a conversion course to learn the American Training Manual which had become the GAF 'bible' and which was followed word for word in the air. The RAF system, where an instructor developed his own style to teach an exercise covering the salient points set out in the training manual (AP 3225) was definitely out.

On reporting to Flights the following morning, I found that the conversion flight was a mixture of GAF and RAF instructors, drawn from the earlier arrivals and now fully converted. I drew an RAF instructor and was introduced to the Harvard Mk. IV. It differed from the RAF Mk II. in that it had a steerable tail wheel locked to the rudder and Automatic Direction Finding (ADF) equipment instead of the SBA of the RAF aeroplanes.

One change from the RAF handling of the Harvard, which met with universal approval, was that take-off and landings were carried out with the aeroplane hoods closed; no longer would the instructor in the rear seat suffer the onslaught of the slipstream. Helmets, goggles and oxygen masks were replaced with headsets. It did make landing from the back seat more difficult, especially at night, but one soon adapted and the conversion proceeded.

The flying was no problem, the only real change in handling was the take-off. The RAF method was to raise the tail early, accepting the tendency for a sharp swing to the left for which the aeroplane was well known. Here the aeroplane would take off in a tail down attitude thus minimising the swing. The rest of the handling and exercise aims were similar to the Mk. II but to present them in what was a stilted manner, following the Manual, meant a considerable rethink. However, all worked out, and by the end of February I was ready to be let loose on the students.

At that time, the student training was split between four airfields – Memmingen, Mengen, Kaufbeuren and Landsberg. I joined a Flight at Landsberg. The composition of the Flights was mixed GAF and RAF, with the RAF in the majority. The Flight Commander was a GAF Captain (Hauptman).

The GAF instructors were generally officers with a small number of NCOs, most of whom had served in the Luftwaffe during the war and were good pilots. Despite having served in opposing air forces, this did not pose a problem and relations were amicable and professional. There were occasional disagreements that were sorted out by compromise on both sides.

Away from work, there was only infrequent social contact. GAF colleagues were scattered around the area with few married quarters and a different lifestyle

In overall command of the training flights was a GAF Major (Squadron Leader). The students were a mixture of officers and NCOs.

The first thing that impressed me when I met my students was their good English. Since English is the international language of aviation, they had been through a language school in their early training and had acquired a good grasp of the language, not just aviation words and phrases. This made instruction in the air relatively simple, particularly as the standard pre-flight briefing was 'read exercise "X" in your manual' which they did. Since the air exercise followed 'the book' closely they were able to understand the instruction given and make steady progress.

I retained the same two students up to the end of their course in June (Hr. Engel and Hr. Hager) and was pleased to see them graduate. Their standard was well up to what would have been expected of an RAF student at that stage. This pattern of training continued as course followed course, for the rest of my tour at Landsberg. The only changes were the venues. Depending on the stage a course had reached, the students were moved between Mengen, Kaufbeuren and Landsberg for night flying.

This continual change of venue posed something of a problem. Kaufbeuren was twenty-five miles from the Kaserne and we drove there daily, but Mengen was seventy miles away and with the early start in the summer (0630), this meant a week away, staying in a local gasthaus or hotel. This certainly improved our level of German, although again many of the local people we met had some English. The proprietor of the gasthaus had been a POW in England for two years.

I did get something of a change in March 1960, when I and another RAF instructor took over a course of students who, after graduation, had been chosen to become instructors. This was a break from the back seat for us and as the course (although based on the 'bible') included some airways navigation, we were able to take them up north to visit RAF Stations where they were able to experience Ground Controlled Approach (GCA) approaches instead of using ADF all the time. It also gave us a chance to show them some aspects of the Harvard in the aerobatic role that they hadn't seen before. This course finished in August and it was then back to another group of students.

When the courses ended, we carried out continuation training (Exercise 60-2 in the GAF) and the Flight Commanders carried out the statutory standardisation checks. Exercise 60-2 was a chance to visit the RAF in the north, particularly

GAF Harvard up from Mengen.

Fougas up from Penzing.

Brüggen and Wildenrath. To get there meant airways flying. With the Harvard having only four VHF radio channels and the airways controllers insisting on our remaining in contact, it entailed going off with a handful of radio crystals. As the channels changed, the unfortunate person in the back seat had to unstrap, turn around and, facing backwards, switch crystals - never a dull moment.

One of the Exercise 60-2 requirements was, once a year, over a weekend, to carry out a long navigation flight, landing away in one of the neighbouring countries. The favourites were usually Denmark (Copenhagen) and the UK (Manston). It meant up to four (plus) hours sitting in a Harvard, and produced surprised faces among ground handling parties when, after having parked a German aeroplane, two RAF officers climbed out.

Our Instrument Rating Examiner (IRE) also took these between-course breaks to update our Instrument Ratings to RAF standard. During each year we also had a visit from one of the RAF doctors from HQ 2nd Tactical Air Force (2nd TAF), to carry out annual medicals.

Leave was the standard RAF forty-two days per year. Landsberg was close to the Austrian and Italian borders and maximum advantage was taken of this. During the winter weekends, it was off skiing at Garmisch-Partenkirchen, the Zugspitze or across to the many Austrian resorts. In the summer, it was Venice and the Italian Riviera. Also, as part of the contract, we were entitled to one paid return trip to the UK.

In early 1961 we were told that the Mission was to be

extended until 1964 and were asked if we wished to remain at Landsberg. Most took the opportunity to extend but some half dozen or so, for a variety of reasons, elected to leave. I was one of those. I had been in Germany for five years and with my Short Service Commission due to expire in 1964, I felt it was time to return to life in the UK.

Coincident with this news, the GAF had begun to introduce jet training for their pilots with the Fouga Magister and conversion was beginning. For good reason, initial priority was given to their own personnel, not least because it meant an upgrade in their pay. However, there were insufficient numbers of them to meet the forecast flying commitment and so we were asked to submit our jet experience to the CO. Those with the most jet flying would be given priority. As it turned out I was among those with the most jet flying hours but, having elected to return home, was not considered.

In April 1961, our replacements began to arrive and in May, my posting arrived. In late May, I handed over my students and spent a final leave in Italy, then it was back to the UK. During my time at Landsberg I had added 600 hours on the Mk. IV (Harvard) to my total of 900 hours on the Mk. II.

It had been an interesting experience to sample the training system of another air force and it undoubtedly worked for its students. It produced a good standard of pilot, but because of the restricted nature of the instruction, there was little scope for individual initiative.

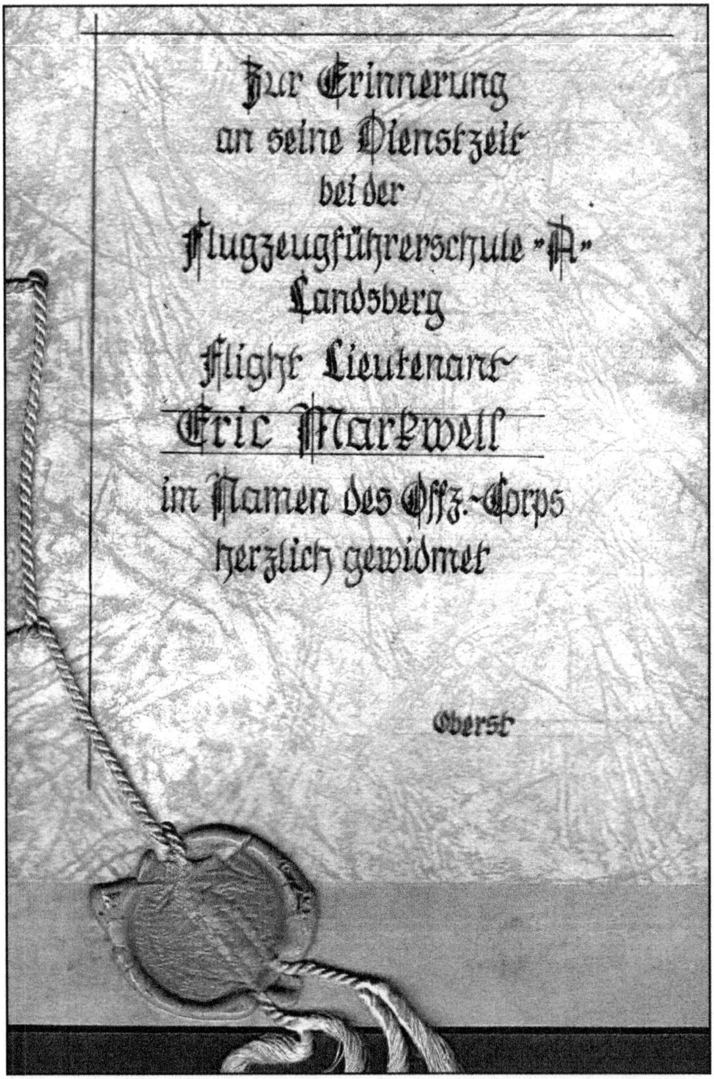

A certificate presented to Eric on leaving the RAF Mission at Landsberg. Translated this reads:
'In memory of your service time at the Flight Leader A School, Landsberg. In the Name of the Officer Corps, Warmly Dedicated, Colonel'.

PART 2
1961 - 2015

ERIC'S LATER
POST-WAR CAREER
AND RETIREMENT

BY ALAN MARKWELL

UNITED KINGDOM

JULY 1961 - APRIL 1965

JULY 1961 - APRIL 1965

1. CAMBRIDGE UAS*
2. HUCKNALL-NOTTINGHAM UAS*
3. UPWOOD
4. BRAMPTON*
5. ODIHAM*

* STATIONS AT WHICH ERIC SERVED

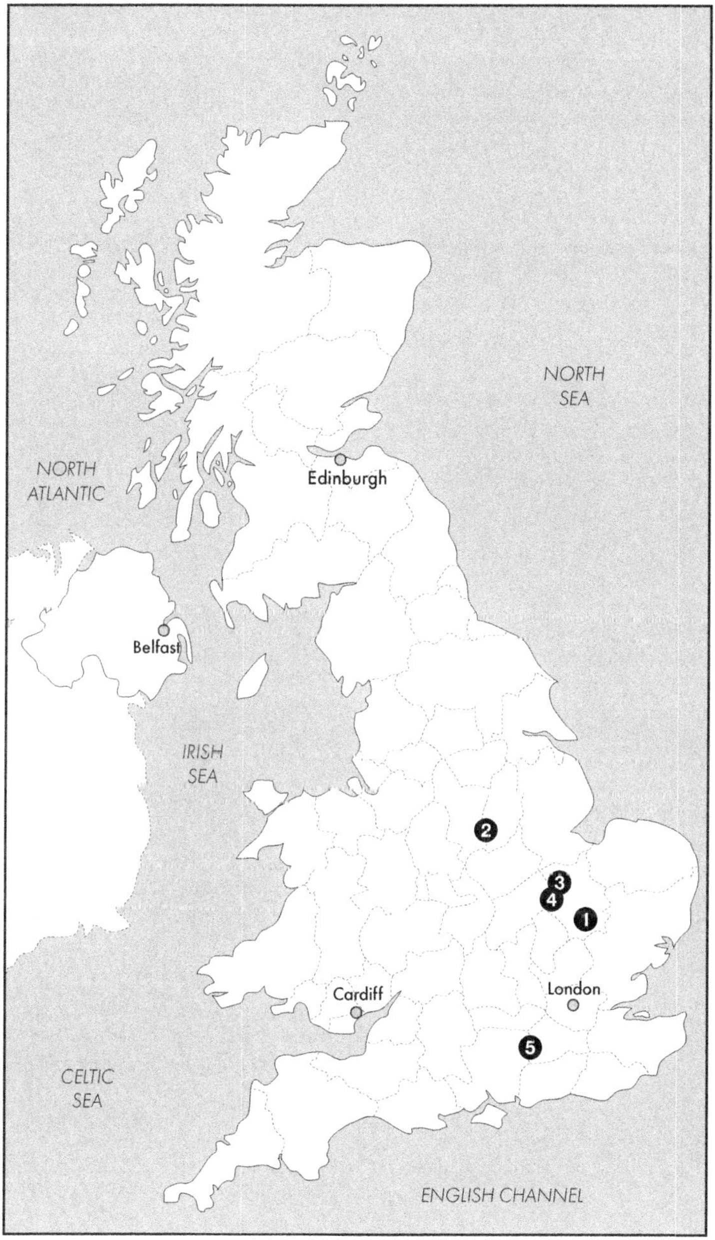
NORTH SEA
NORTH ATLANTIC
Edinburgh
Belfast
IRISH SEA
2
3
4
1
Cardiff
London
5
CELTIC SEA
ENGLISH CHANNEL

CHAPTER 15

RETURNING TO THE UK ONCE MORE

Eric and his family returned to England in July 1961, flying back across the Channel on Silver City Airways in a Bristol Freighter.

Eric and the family stayed briefly in Hucknall, waiting for a married quarter to become available at RAF Brampton where Eric had been posted to the Joint Air Reconnaissance Intelligence Centre (JARIC) as a Photographic Interpreter (PI). Whilst waiting for this, Eric had a brief period of instructing at the Nottingham and Cambridge University Air Squadron (UAS), prior to a PI course at Upwood and settling into the job at JARIC. By this time his logbook shows a total of 3,524 hours.

At the end of his time at JARIC, posting loomed (again, Eric hated being desk bound) and he spent the November and December of 1964 at Manby on a refresher course, flying the Varsity. This was prior to a two-month stint, starting in February

1965 at Odiham, converting to the Twin Pioneer. At this time, Eric and his wife also bought their house in Brampton, which was eventually to become their retirement home.

In March 1965, Eric received a posting to 78 Squadron at Khormaksar (Aden), on Twin Pioneers. This posting was cancelled and immediately replaced by a posting to Linton, only to have that also rescinded and replaced by a posting to 209 Squadron, flying Twin and Single Pioneers from Seletar, Singapore.

With that, the family was off, flying from Heathrow via Tehran and Bombay, arriving twenty-seven hours later on a British Eagle Britannia, G-AOVB (Endeavour).[7]

7 See *Historical Context* section, page 235, for more informaton.

Eric's Ford Consul being loaded at Le Touquet for the return from Germany.

British Eagle International Airline tickets to Singapore.

G-AOVB at Heathrow.

SOUTH EAST ASIA

APRIL 1965 - MARCH 1968

APRIL 1965 - MARCH 1968

1. SELETAR*

2. LABUAN* & BRUNEI

3. KUCHING*

4. BARIO*

5. BUTTERWORTH*

6. KOTA TINGGI*

* STATIONS AT WHICH ERIC SERVED

(ROTATE MAP TO VIEW)

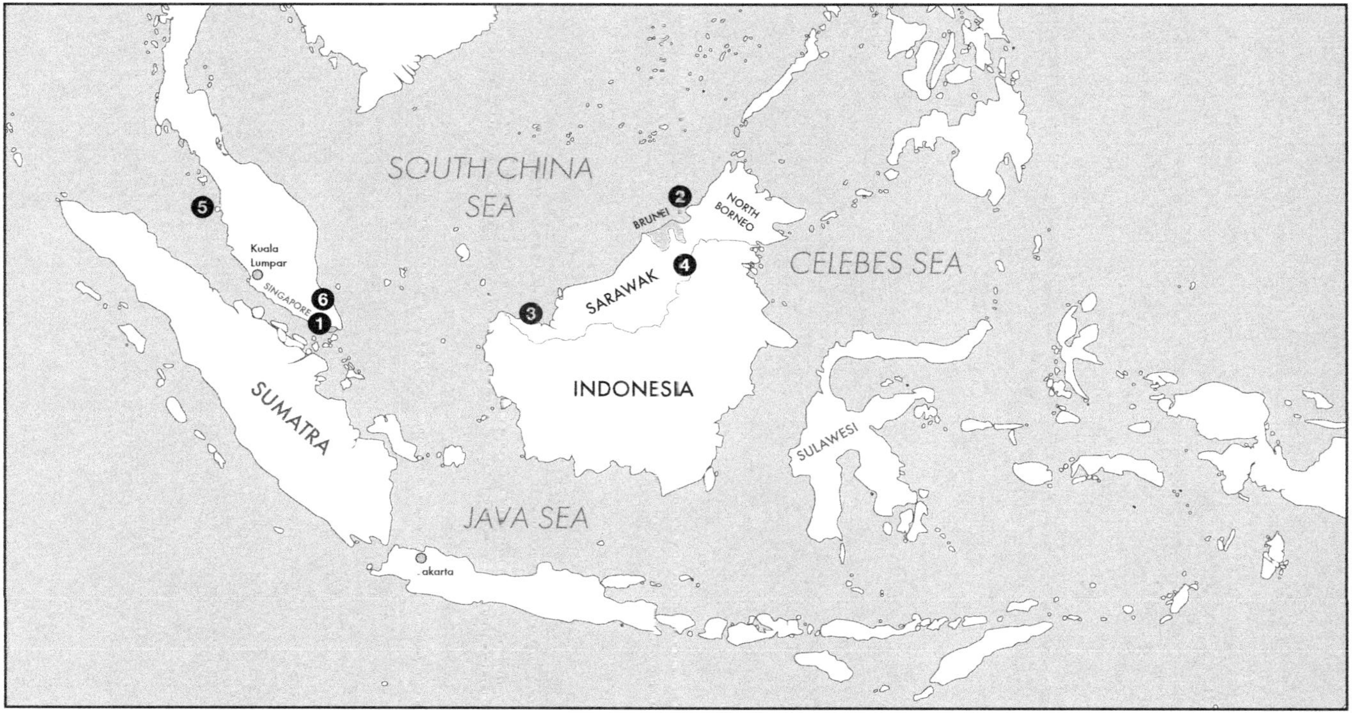
SOUTH CHINA SEA
CELEBES SEA
JAVA SEA
NORTH BORNEO
BRUNEI
SARAWAK
INDONESIA
SULAWESI
SUMATRA
Kuala Lumpar
SINGAPORE
akarta
1
2
3
4
5
6

CHAPTER 16

209 SQUADRON, SINGAPORE

At the time Eric and his family arrived in Singapore on 24th April 1965, there was still a state of confrontation with Indonesia. Eric joined 209 Squadron, part of the Far East Air Force (FEAF) tasked with supporting the army in Malaya and Borneo, often flying in to strips that were literally hacked out of the jungle. Eric's logbook records his conversion to the strips commencing as soon as he joined 209 (for example, eight landings at Pengerang in Malaya on 17th May). Further afield, there were detachments to Labuan, Kuching, Brunei and Kota Tinggi.

In August and September 1965, between Twin Pioneer trips, Eric added the Single Pioneer to his type ratings, with twenty-four hours and fifteen minutes flying and 112 landings to complete the conversion. In spite of its fuel tank wing, the Single Pioneer did not have the range to reach Borneo from Seletar. Thus all of 209's pilots had to qualify for carrier landings in order that the aeroplane could be ferried to destinations

Preparing for departure at Fort Tapong with the Commander.

Eric on the log bridge constructed across the river at Fort Tapong.

Eric's sons with the Commander at Fort Kemar.

Tea on the terrace, Fort Kemar.

beyond their normal range. Eric's turn came on 18th July 1966, when he landed on HMS Albion (four landings and take-offs). With its outstanding short field performance, the aeroplane was readily suited to carrier operation for transportation purposes, although without arrestor gear, Eric commented that it was a fair-weather carrier operation only.

As the reader may imagine, things such as health and safety were very different in those far-off days. In August 1966, Eric flew a detachment to Butterworth, Malaya in Twin Pioneer XM957. Taking the opportunity for a holiday in Penang, he took his family with him. Despite much resistance from his wife, his sons were delighted when he announced that he was taking them with him and his Navigator, Flight Lieutenant George Angus, in '957' on a routine supply trip around two of the jungle forts that they supplied. On 22nd August, they flew from Butterworth to Fort Kemar, on to Fort Tapong and then returned to Butterworth. It was a never-to-be-forgotten experience. Fort Kemar was commanded by a Malay Captain who treated Eric and his two sons to tea on the terrace. Fort Tapong was commanded by a Sikh Commander – Bhagwan Singh.

It's fair to say that they were treated like royalty, and were shown around the forts, including the log bridge, built to cross the river at Tapong. For Eric's sons, this was a once-in-a-lifetime experience that one couldn't conceive happening in this day and age. The only downside to the day was that Eric got a royal telling off from his wife Georgie when they returned, very late. With no mobile phones available in those days, they had been completely out of touch and unreachable.

On 1st February 1967, 209 Squadron celebrated its 50th Anniversary. A look at the squadron crest shows a falling red eagle. Whilst there still exists controversy to this day, as to whether the Red Baron, Rittmeister Manfred von Richthofen, was brought down by ground fire or by Captain Roy Brown of 9 Squadron (which became 209 Squadron), 209 Squadron has always claimed the victory, hence the crest.

As part of the celebrations, for the Mess party, the squadron engineers built an approximately five-eighth scale Fokker Triplane that took pride of place. The rumour was that the scale was driven by the pram wheels that were used, with the rest of the model scaled from them!

This was also the time of the Schultz cartoon strip 'Snoopy vs. the Red Baron'. With permission from Charles Schultz, the unofficial squadron patch and shoulder patch became 'Snoopy on his Dog House' (Eric's patch is shown on page 185). The aeroplanes also started to sport a small white circle with a red falling eagle on the fins plus dayglo Snoopy stickers.

During his time on 209, Eric progressed from Pilot to (once again) QFI (1st October 1965) and finally to Wing Examiner (1st January 1968). He also gained promotion to Squadron Leader on 1st January 1968 and was awarded the Queen's Commendation for Valuable Service in the Air (QCVSA).

Eric often spoke of his time on 209 and maintained that it was some of the most interesting flying he ever did. Once away

209 Sqn. Standard at 50th Anniversary celebrations.

The Fokker Triplane replica built for the celebrations.

Twin Pioneer XL997 at Seletar open day 26th February 1967.

Eric, somewhere over the jungle.

from base, they were very much on their own. They flew with a navigator (there being few navigational aids) and where necessary they re-fuelled with a hand pump from fifty-five gallon drums.

In September 1967 Eric added two hours and fifty-five minutes as Second Pilot in a Beverley (XB262) and in October added one hour and five minutes familiarisation on a Beaver (XP814).

Sadly, all good things come to an end. Eric's last trip with 209 Squadron was in Single Pioneer XL666 on 7th March 1968, bringing his Far East Air Force time to a close with 550 hours, 25 minutes Twin Pioneer and 266 hours, 5 minutes of Single Pioneer flying. As he said, it was some of the most interesting and rewarding flying he ever did.

Single Pioneer XL705 at Bario.

Eric's Snoopy patch.

Eric and his cousin Gwen, whom he visited in Montreal during his training in Canada. This picture was taken sometime in the mid 1970s.

UNITED KINGDOM

MARCH 1968 - FEB 1978

MARCH 1968 - FEB 1978

1. MANBY*
2. OAKINGTON*
3. BRAMPTON*
4. HIGH WYCOMBE*
5. LEEMING*

* STATIONS AT WHICH ERIC SERVED

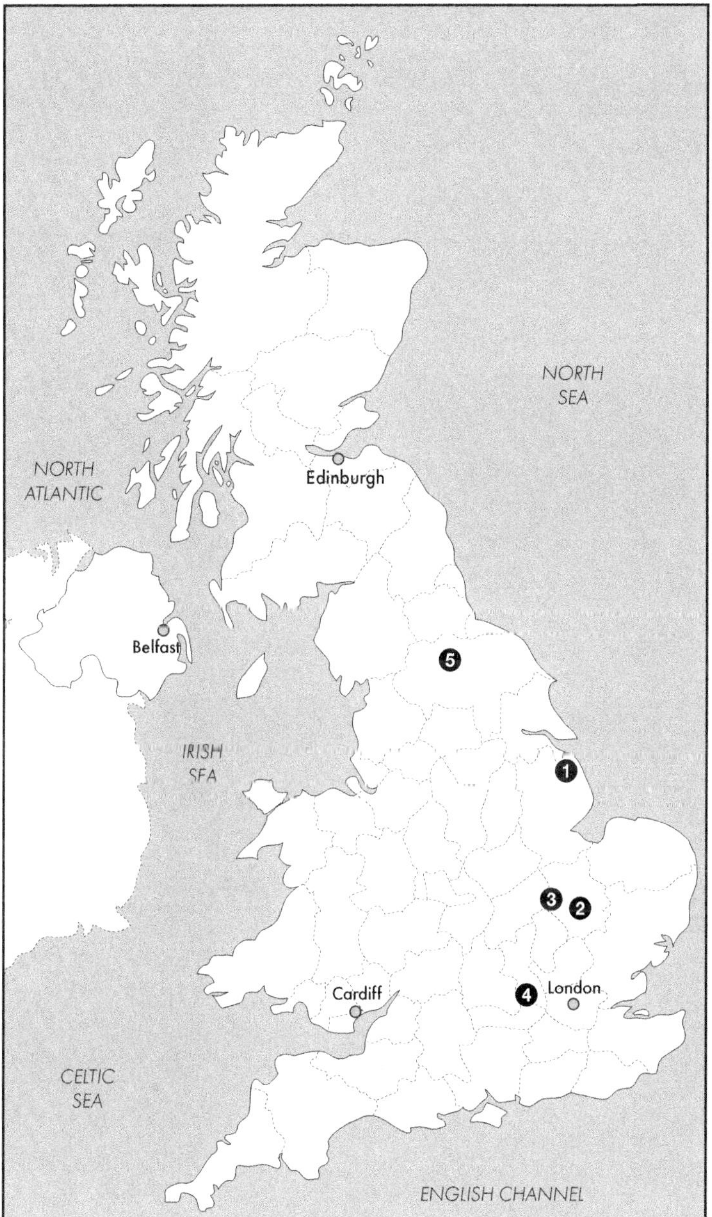
NORTH SEA
NORTH ATLANTIC
Edinburgh
Belfast
5
IRISH SEA
1
3
2
4
London
Cardiff
CELTIC SEA
ENGLISH CHANNEL

CHAPTER 17

OAKINGTON (NO. 5 FTS) AND THE JETSTREAM

Eric and his family returned from Singapore to a grey, cold England on 20th March 1968. Eric had been posted to No. 5 FTS at Oakington with, once again, a refresher course (twenty-nine hours and forty-five minutes) on the Varsity at Manby, prior to taking up the posting at Oakington on 1st July.

From a family perspective, this worked well since they were able to return to the Brampton home that Eric and Georgie had purchased just prior to leaving for Singapore. Eric remained at Oakington until the end of 1974, so completing two tours split by an eleven-month stint at HQ Strike Command, High Wycombe. As part of his duties during that 11 months Eric was responsible for the RAF presence at the annual Earls Court Boat Show (the RAF showcased Maritime Reconnaissance, Search and Rescue) and thus was responsible for escorting the then Prime Minister Edward Heath around the exhibit.

During this period, Eric clocked up 1,384 hours, 35 minutes on the Varsity, and spent familiarisation time on the Bassett (the RAF name for the Beagle 206), registration XS770, which was nicknamed the 'Regal Beagle' – the aeroplane in which King Charles III (when the Prince of Wales), gained his twin rating.

In March 1974, the first of the new Jetstreams XX476 arrived and Eric became the Project Pilot for the Jetstream Project Group, spending some time at Prestwick where the aeroplanes were built.

The aeroplane had been designed by Handley Page but the programme was acquired by Scottish Aviation when Handley Page declared bankruptcy. In turn Scottish Aviation was absorbed into British Aerospace in 1977. Eric came to know John Blair, the Chief Test Pilot, very well and during one of his visits was familiarised with the other Scottish Aviation product of the time, the Bulldog. Through this friendship, Eric and his family were kindly invited to the Farnborough Air Show and to the Scottish Aviation Chalet where, amongst all the other displays, they watched John display the Bulldog in his usual polished fashion.

Eric flew 189 hours, 20 minutes on the Jetstream at Oakington. His last flight was on 31st December 1974 when the Station closed and the Jetstreams moved to Leeming.

On 2nd January 1975, Eric's logbook for that time is endorsed by the CFI:

Eric escorting UK Prime Minister, Edward Heath, at the Earl's Court Boat Show.

Varsity WF331, Oakington, August 1968.

Eric in the cockpit of the Liberator at Duxford.

Taxiing a Jetstream with the port engine shut down and the propeller feathered.

'Assessment of Ability: Well above the Average
Remarks: Varsity and Jetstream A2
Standardisation QFI.
Thank you, Eric, for your magnificent work in
introducing the Jetstream at Oakington.'

Eric was posted to HQ Training Command at Brampton. This was a desk job which as we know, Eric hated. Somehow, he kept his hand in through October 1976 flying sixteen hours and twenty-five minutes as Second Pilot on the Dominie and adding one further hour on the Varsity at Finningley.

There was one highlight in mid-1975. Eric had come to know the curator of the then nascent, now world-famous, Imperial War Museum (IWM) Duxford and through this connection was re-united with the Liberator.

Post-war, the RAF had left most of the Liberators it had used in India rendering them (so it was thought) 'scrap' by cutting the main spars. However, the Indian Air Force had re-furbished and continued to use them. When they finally left service, in the mid 1970s, at least one was acquired by an American collector. This aeroplane staged through Duxford on its way to the USA. Eric was privileged to gain access to the aeroplane, sitting in the Captain's seat once again – the first time in twenty-nine years.

In October 1976, Eric had a refresher multi-engine course with the RAF Training Flight at the College of Air Training in Hamble. This was preparation for re-joining the Jetstream Project on the CFS Exam Wing at Leeming, which he did at the end of the month.

Eric leading the Training Command Grouping at the Silver Jubilee Review.

Eric returning from his final RAF Flight.

Celebrating after his final RAF Flight on 20th January 1978.

Eric being towed by colleagues.

Retirement!

Eric's time at Leeming included two rather differing highlights. The first was an engine shutdown, resulting in an asymmetric landing on 19th April (this was the second asymmetric landing Eric had in the Jetstream, the first being at Oakington).

The second and rather more of a highlight was leading the Training Command section for Her Majesty Queen Elizabeth II's Silver Jubilee Review on 29th July in XX492. Eric's logbook shows practice on 21st and 27th July, the Review on 29th July and Finningley Open Day on 30th.

This was perhaps a fitting highlight to Eric's last year of service. On 10th January 1978 he made his last RAF sortie in XX498, bringing a thirty-five year RAF career to a close with a total of 6,436 hours, 50 minutes across thirty-five different types, a number unlikely to be exceeded today.

Eric's last day of service was 13th February 1978. A celebration was laid on by his colleagues which, besides a Mess party, consisted largely of towing him around the Station in his greatcoat and a bowler hat to signify his 'civvy' status.

Eric's logbook was signed off on 13th January with the comment:

'Good Luck, Best Wishes and Many Thanks'

Through his last few months at Leeming, Eric had gained his civilian ratings and qualified as Type Rating Examiner (TRE) and Instrument Rating Examiner (IRE). This opened the door to the Civilian Aviation Authority Flying Unit (CAAFU) which Eric joined in March 1978.

CHAPTER 18

CIVIL AVIATION AUTHORITY FLYING UNIT (CAAFU) AND THURSTON AVIATION

Initially Eric was detached from Stansted (where CAAFU was based) to Cranfield, returning in July 1979. During this time, Eric became acquainted with lighter aviation types such as the Cessna 150 and 172, and the light twins such as the Dove and PA23 Aztec.

Eric spent five years with CAAFU, adding many light singles and twins to his logbook – in order to examine on a type, the CAAFU staff had first to convert to it. Two types which were of particular interest and which re-acquainted him with four-engine types were the DH Sea Heron and the C130 (on which he examined RAF pilots for instrument ratings). During his time at CAAFU, Eric added 1,483 hours to his logbook.

Whilst at Stansted with CAAFU, Eric had become friendly with Eric Thurston whose company, Thurston Aviation, was

Retiring: Cabair at Cranfield.

Retiring: with CAAFU.

Eric's favourite - Beech King Air 200 G-IPRA.

located a stone's throw away from the CAAFU building.

Eric retired from CAAFU on 30th December 1983 and joined Thurston Aviation flying what would now be called air-taxi or executive-hire operations. During this period, Eric added several more types, but his favourite was the Beech King Air.

Much of his time at Thurston was spent flying King Air G-IPRA which was used extensively under charter by the heart transplant team at Papworth Hospital. A typical sortie would start with a call in the early hours, to get the aeroplane from Stansted over to Cambridge to pick up the team. They would then fly to a destination in Europe and return with a heart for the transplant patient in a special container. Everyone involved understood the critical time limits for these flights. Eric recalled some 'hairy' trips that required help from the excellent Cambridge controllers when returning to land in bad weather, as well as a trip into Heathrow where the controllers allowed them to 'jump the queue' by using the cross runway. This was runway 05/23 which is no longer used and I believe the heart was destined for Harefield Hospital, hence the use of Heathrow. A number of these trips included the eminent heart surgeon Professor (now Sir) Magdi Yacoub.

Eric flew with Thurston Aviation until December 1991 with his last flight on 3rd December (in PA34 G-FILE). So ended a remarkable career with 10,797 hours, 15 minutes on sixty-four different aeroplane types (eighty-one if sub-types are included).

Sadly, Eric died on 20th October 2015. Writing his eulogy, I referred to him as part of the 'Greatest Generation', a phrase that Americans use when talking about their Second World War veterans. In his modest way, Eric was truly part of that remarkable generation, the likes of which we will never see again.

APPENDICES

GLOSSARY OF TERMS

A/A	Anti-Aircraft
ACDC	Aircrew Dispersal Centre
ACHU	Aircrew Holding Unit
ACRC	Aircrew Reception Centre
ADF	Automatic Direction Finding
A/G	Air Gunner
APU	Auxiliary Power Unit
ARP	Air Raid Precautions
ATC	Air Training Corps
ATT	Anti-tetanus Inoculation
BAFO	British Air Forces of Occupation
BCATP	British Commonwealth Air Training Plan
BOAC	British Overseas Airways Corporation
BOQ	Bachelor Officer Quarter
CAAFU	Civil Aviation Authority Flying Unit
CASEVAC	Casualty Evacuation
CFI	Chief Flying Instructor
CFS	Central Flying School
CNR	Canadian National Railway
CO	Commanding Officer

CPR	Canadian Pacific Railway
CRT	Cathode Ray Tube
CT	Communist Terrorist
DH	De Havilland (see '*Types Flown*')
DI	Drill Instructor
EATS	Empire Air Training Scheme
ECFS	Empire Central Flying School
EFTS	Elementary Flying Training School
FE	Flight Engineer
FEAF	Far East Air Force
FFI	Free from infection
F/O	Flying Officer
FTS	Flying Training School
GAF	German Air Force
GCA	Ground Controlled Approach
GRS	Ground Reconnaissance School
HCU	Heavy Conversion Unit
HF	High Frequency
HMS	His/Her Majesty's Ship
IRE	Instrument Rating Examiner
ITW	Initial Training Wing
IWM	Imperial War Museum
JARIC	Joint Air Reconnaissance Intelligence Centre
LAC	Leading Aircraftman
MF	Medium Frequency
MO	Medical Officer
MOD	Ministry of Defence

MRLA	Malayan Races Liberation Army
NAAFI	Navy, Army and Air Force Institute
NATO	North Atlantic Treaty Organisation
NCO	Non-Commissioned Officer
ORB	Operational Record Book
OTU	Operational Training Unit
PD	Personnel Depot
PDC	Personnel Despatch Centre
PEI	Prince Edward Island
PI	Photographic Interpreter
PNB	Pilot / Navigator / Air Bomber
P/O	Pilot Officer
POW	Prisoner of War
PRC	Personnel Reception Centre (also know as Personnel Receiving Centre)
PT	Physical Training
PTI	Physical Training Instructor
QCVSA	Queen's Commendation for Valuable Service in the Air
QFI	Qualified Flying Instructor
RAF	Royal Air Force
RAFVR	RAF Volunteer Reserve
RCAF	Royal Canadian Air Force
RFU	Refresher Flying Unit
RR	Rolls Royce (see '*Types Flown*')
RTO	Railway Transport Officer
SBA	Standard Beam Approach

SEAC	South East Asia Command
SFTS	Service Flying Training School
SIO	Station Intelligence Officer
SNCO	Senior Non-Commissioned Officer
SP	Sergeant Pilot
STOL	Short Take-Off and Landing
TAB	Typhoid and Paratyphoid Inoculation
TAF	Tactical Air Force
TRE	Type Rating Examiner
UAS	University Air Squadron
USAF	United States Air Force
U/T	Under Training
VE	Victory in Europe
VHF	Very High Frequency
VJ	Victory over Japan
VR	Volunteer Reserve
WD	Women's Division (also War Department)
W/O	Warrant Officer
W/Op	Wireless Operator

HISTORICAL CONTEXT

Eric's flying life spans many momentous events in world history that provide a backdrop to this narrative, even if those events don't readily spring from its pages. These historical notes are my attempt, as Eric's son, to put my father's life into the context of what was happening in the world at a particular time and give the reader some background to Eric's flying and travels.

CHAPTER 2:

ENLISTMENT - PAGE 15

AIRCREW RECEPTION CENTRE
LORD'S CRICKET GROUND

By the end of 1940, as part of the huge expansion of the Armed Forces, it was recognised that existing RAF recruitment facilities could not cope and that a new recruit reception centre would be needed. All sporting fixtures had been cancelled so, to cope with the ever-increasing number of recruits, Lord's Cricket Ground in Marylebone, London and surrounding blocks of flats were requisitioned to serve as the Aircrew Reception Centre (ACRC). A plaque on the Lord's pavilion commemorates this.

CHAPTER 4:

PROFESSIONAL TRAINING - PAGE 35

THE BRITISH COMMONWEALTH AIR TRAINING PLAN (BCATP)

With war clouds gathering and recognising the need to train vast numbers of aircrew, the British and Commonwealth Air Training Plan or Empire Air Training Scheme (EATS) was set up in 1939 by Great Britain, Canada, New Zealand and Australia. In doing so it was recognised that to stand any chance of success, the training would have to be dispersed and carried out well away from potential conflict zones.

Under the agreement, which called for the training of approximately 50,000 aircrew a year for the duration of the war, the crews received elementary training in Canada and other Commonwealth countries such as Rhodesia or South Africa, with more advanced training carried out in Canada.

Canada was particularly suitable for such training, with its abundance of air space well away from the Luftwaffe and the Japanese Navy. The first recruits joined the programme on 29th April 1940 and the BCATP ran until 31st March 1945.

The Canadian Prime Minister, William Mackenzie King, was initially cautious regarding the scheme but after agreement was reached on the BCATP on 17th December 1939, he became an enthusiastic supporter in the belief that Canada had secured a critical role which did not require a huge land army (apparently, Mackenzie King was mindful of the vast number of Canadian casualties during the First World War).

The Plan had been a challenge to negotiate; Canada had agreed to accept most of the costs associated with it but insisted that Britain consent to the training taking precedence over all other aspects of the Canadian war effort. The British had expected that whatever their origin, all graduates of the scheme would become members of the Royal Air Force, however King insisted that Canadian graduates would remain members of the Royal Canadian Air Force and be identified as such.

As can be imagined, the programme required a huge logistical effort and number of people to run it. Once announced, towns and cities across Canada lobbied the government to be selected as a location for a BCATP base. At that time, much of Canada still had economies that had been devastated by the Great

Depression, so a base meant construction jobs followed by waves of trainees, staff with wages to spend and jobs for local people.

A feature of the programme was the welcome given to the trainees, most of whom were thousands of miles from home and had never been out of their respective countries. Many Canadians welcomed trainees into their homes, life-long friendships and marriages sometimes being the result. Eric refers to the hospitality shown to him and some of his fellow trainees.

The BCATP was controlled by Canada to an overall policy and standard set by the RAF, the training being carried out by the RCAF and supported by various commercial companies. At its peak, there were 107 schools with approximately 104,000 staff and over 10,000 aeroplanes! As noted, the Canadian government largely footed the bill, eventually paying about three quarters of the total cost which amounted to some CA$3 billion. By the time the Plan ended in 1945, over 130,000 people had graduated not only as pilots but also navigators, bomb aimers, wireless operators and air gunners. They came not only from the four founding nations but also from the USA and many of the countries overrun by the Nazis including Poland, Czechoslovakia, Norway, Belgium, the Netherlands and France.

President Roosevelt probably summed up the effort in the best way calling Canada: 'The Aerodrome of Democracy'.

CHAPTER 4:

PROFESSIONAL TRAINING - PAGE 35

THE BATTLE OF THE ATLANTIC

When Eric crossed the Atlantic in June 1943, the Battle of the Atlantic had been raging for more than three years. The battle is generally recognised as the longest single campaign of the Second World War, arguably beginning in September 1939 when Germany invaded Poland and war was declared, right through to the capitulation of Germany on 8th May 1945. During the war, all the major liners, including the SS Île de France, were commandeered and converted into troop transports. As Eric ruefully comments, the luxury cabins, used pre-war by the rich and famous, had been stripped out and only basic facilities remained. However, the ships were fast for their day and used to cross the Atlantic un-escorted whereas most merchant shipping was organised into conveys escorted by the navies of Great Britain, Canada and the USA.

The Battle of the Atlantic was a contest between the Allies and the Axis powers (Germany in reality) for control of the Atlantic. Britain's survival and its ability to continue the war depended on supplies of food, fuel, aeroplanes and military vehicles from the USA and Canada. In Churchill's view the Battle of the Atlantic was the greatest threat to the nation's survival at that time.

The battle was fought in three phases. The first comparatively short phase covered nearly a year - the period from the outbreak of war through to the fall of France in June 1940. During this period, the Allies practically held superiority over the waves and drove German merchant shipping from the seas, establishing an effective blockade of supplies to Germany, although the Kriegsmarine (German Navy) did attempt to inflict damage to the Allied shipping.

The second phase began when Germany overran the Low Countries and France, giving them access to Atlantic ports. Prior to this the U-boats and surface raiders had to take the long route from Germany's northern ports through the Denmark Strait south of Iceland and onward into the Atlantic. Britain lost French naval support (Britain controversially sank much of the French fleet at Mers-El-Kebir on the coast of French Algeria on 3rd July 1940) and had incurred naval losses following the disastrous Norwegian campaign and the retreat from Dunkirk. Gaining access to the French Atlantic ports gave Germany a realistic chance to starve Britain out of the war. Germany's major surface raiders and U-boats were dramatically successful.

By 1941 the Allies had introduced the fully-escorted convoy system. Although the USA was technically a non-belligerent (supporting Britain but not directly involved in military operations), a deal between Britain and the USA was made. Through this, the USA gained leases on bases in Newfoundland and the Caribbean and gave Britain fifty destroyers to assist in making good its losses and as convoy escorts. Canada also built naval and air bases in Newfoundland and by the end of 1941, despite its 'neutrality', the USA was engaged in escorting shipping along its northeast coast alongside the Canadians and British.

The USA formally entered the Second World War in December 1941, with the Japanese attack on the US naval base at Pearl Harbour. This opened up previously 'off limits' waters to the U-boats which mounted a massive campaign. The result of this was that Allied shipping losses spiked in early 1942. In response, and considered to be Phase 3 of the Battle of the Atlantic, the first convoys in the US Zone were established initially by the Canadians and later by the Americans. Transatlantic convoys also shifted their western terminus from Halifax to New York, which is the reason for Eric arriving in New York rather than Nova Scotia. Throughout 1942, the convoy system continued to be strengthened and it had also forced the U-boats back into the mid-Atlantic. However, a lapse in the Ultra[8] intelligence (by which the Allies were reading the U-boat radio traffic) gave the U-boats a temporary advantage with Germany attacking every major convoy.

At the Casablanca Conference in the spring of 1943, an agreement was reached by Roosevelt, Churchill and Stalin, to pump resources into the Atlantic war. Escort carriers, improved radar systems and long-range aeroplanes such as the Liberator (in which Eric was later to go to war) closed the mid-Atlantic gap, thus finally providing continuous air cover. This resulted in a major defeat for the U-boats from which they never fully recovered. That said, U-boats continued to wage a guerrilla campaign that by its nature was unpredictable. Against this background, Eric and his companions crossed the Atlantic.

---

8 Ultra was the name given to intelligence derived from top secret work at Bletchley Park where the code-breakers (perhaps the most well-known being Alan Turing) had successfully decrypted German coded messages sent from cipher machines, the best known of which was Enigma.

CHAPTER 11

TRAVEL TO INDIA - PAGE 115

THE WAR IN THE FAR EAST AND THE FORGOTTEN ARMY

The war in the Far East ran from 7th December 1941, with the Japanese attack on the US naval base at Pearl Harbour and the invasion of Indo-China. Sir Winston Churchill called the fall of Singapore on 15th February 1942: 'the worst disaster and largest capitulation in British history'.

The South East Asian theatre of the Second World War was the name given to the campaign of the Pacific War in Burma, India, Thailand, the Philippines, Indo-China, Malaya and Singapore.

Singapore had long been the major British base in South East Asia and was key to British military planning for the defence of the British Empire in that part of the world. Yet despite the debacle of Pearl Harbour, where the Japanese attacked the US Navy and brought the US into the war, Singapore was held to be impregnable. The problem was the traditional military thinking that assumed an attack from the sea and had therefore set up most of its defences facing outwards, largely ignoring the land approach from the Malayan peninsula.

The Japanese army invaded Indo-China and headed south for Malaya on the same day as the Pearl Harbour attack. The conventional British military thinking at the time had concluded that the jungles of Malaya were impenetrable and that the Japanese were an inferior fighting force whereas the converse was true; the Japanese were skilled at jungle warfare. It took barely two months for the Japanese to conquer Malaya and Singapore and then turn their attention to Siam, now called Thailand and Burma, now called Myanmar. By June 1942 the British, Indian and Chinese forces had been driven out of both Thailand and Burma and the Japanese army was threatening India.

After the surrender of Singapore on 15th February 1942, the tens of thousands of Allied prisoners were subjected to a brutal regime of violence, callous neglect and forced labour. From 1942, many of the prisoners were forced to build the Burma-Thailand railway, which became known as the 'Death Railway' due to its high mortality rate. Over 100,000 Allied prisoners and civilian labourers died during the sixteen-month construction of the railway between 1942 and 1943. The railway was intended to support the build-up of Japanese forces for an attack on India, the supply lines having been severely stretched.

By mid 1943, the Allies had re-grouped and formed the 14th Army under the command of Lieutenant-General William Joseph Slim (usually known as Bill Slim). A multi-national force comprising units from Commonwealth countries as well as the British and Indian armies, the 14th Army's task was to re-take Burma from the Japanese. Slim's leadership combined effective defensive tactics with imaginative and daring offensives. He was immensely popular with the Indian, Gurkha and British troops under his command. Additionally, from February 1943, British and Nepalese Gurkha troops began mounting long distance raids behind Japanese lines. These troops, special operations units of the British and Indian armies, were officially titled 'Long Range Penetration Groups' but more commonly known as 'Chindits'. Commanded by the deeply eccentric Brigadier Orde Wingate, the Chindits were to become a thorn in the side of the Japanese.

By November 1943, South East Asia Command (SEAC), which replaced India Command, was formed under Lord Louis Mountbatten, Supreme Allied Commander, South East Asia Command and the prosecution of the war against the Japanese entered a new phase. In March 1944, the Japanese attacked India's northeastern frontier in an attempt to forestall the impending Allied invasion and liberation of Burma. The Japanese intention was to cut the road to Imphal and Kohima, interrupt supplies to China and capture British bases on the

Imphal plain. Despite fierce fighting, by April Imphal and Kohima had been cut off.

The battles for Kohima and Imphal are recognised now as a turning point in the British war effort in the Far East. At Kohima, a small force of around 1,500 men held a definitive position centred on a garrison hill facing 15,000 Japanese soldiers. Supported by air-dropped supplies, the garrison fought back Japanese advances until it was finally relieved, by which time the Allied troops held an area little more than 350 square metres at the top of the hill. Although fighting continued in the area, the opening of the road at Kohima cleared the way for the relief of Imphal. The Japanese army lost around 60,000 men and began to retreat allowing General Slim's army to begin re-taking Burma.

Eric arrived in India on 27th March 1945 when the war in Europe was nearly over. Although the Japanese were being pushed back on all fronts of the war in the Far East, they were still a ferocious fighting force that preferred death to surrender and the war there was far from over. As we see from Eric's narrative, the operations were challenging in respect of both the conditions in which they operated and the distances flown. It is often said by the veterans of the war in the Far East, in particular following VE day on 8th May 1945 and the end of the war in Europe, that they were the 'Forgotten Army' or the 'Forgotten Air Force'.

Following the turning point at Kohima, and after much fierce fighting, Mandalay and Meiktila were captured in

March 1945 with Rangoon following in May. SEAC then planned for landings in Malaya and Singapore which were overtaken by the Japanese surrender in August 1945 following the dropping of the two atomic bombs on Hiroshima and Nagasaki.

CHAPTER 12

159 SQUADRON - PAGE 118

LEND-LEASE

Lend-Lease was a programme introduced by US President Franklin D. Roosevelt to support the USA's allies (initially Great Britain) whilst recognising the commitment made to the electorate and to keep the USA out of the Second World War. Introduced to Congress on 19th January 1941, the Lend-Lease programme provided for the USA to lend arms to Britain (and subsequently other allies such as Russia) with the understanding that the USA would be paid back in kind after the war. Congress overwhelmingly accepted the plan, with the exception of staunch Isolationists. For Roosevelt this helped resolve two issues: the desperate situation of the British economy and its ability to pay for the aeroplanes, military vehicles, ships and supplies to prosecute the war, and Roosevelt's need to avoid the USA entering the conflict. Of course, this changed after the Japanese attack on the US naval base at Pearl Harbour on 7th December 1941. The Lend-Lease programme continued throughout the Second World War, eventually totalling around US$50 billion to Britain, Russia and thirty-seven other countries. The Liberators that Eric flew in India were supplied as part of this programme.

CHAPTER 13

FINAL DAYS OF SERVICE AND RETURN TO ENGLAND - PAGE 146

THE COLD WAR AND GERMANY

In the closing months of the Second World War, the Allied 2nd Tactical Air Force (2nd TAF) swept across Germany in support of Field Marshal Montgomery's 21st Army Group. 2nd TAF had been equipped and trained in close support of the army. Following the surrender of Germany in May 1945, its role abruptly changed to that of an occupying power. To cope with the changes needed in the transition from an offensive role to one of an occupying power, the British Air Forces of Occupation (BAFO) was formed under Air Chief Marshall

Sir William Sholto Douglas with four groups and sixty-eight squadrons spread across Germany and the Low Countries. However, by the end of 1947, with the post-war British economy struggling, BAFO was drastically downsized to ten squadrons based at just three airfields.

Following decisions taken at the Yalta Conference in February 1945 between Roosevelt, Churchill and Stalin, post-war Germany had been divided by the Allies (as they were at the time) into four sectors that became known as the British, French, US and Soviet zones. Additionally, Berlin, which had been taken by the Soviet Russians in the last days of the war, was divided into four sectors similarly controlled but buried deep within the Soviet Zone.

Post-war, the uneasy Allied coalition deteriorated with mistrust on both sides, perhaps culminating in Sir Winston Churchill's famous speech at Fulton, Missouri, USA on 5th March 1946 with the line: 'From Stettin in the Baltic to Trieste in the Adriatic, an iron curtain has descended across the continent'. Although the term 'iron curtain' had been around for a while, it was this speech that set the tone as to how the democratic Western nations viewed the communist East and is considered by many to be the start of the Cold War between the Western powers and the communist dominated nations.

It was Berlin that was to become the first trial of strength between the two ideologies. On 24th June 1948, the Soviet authorities closed all the road and rail links to Berlin, blockading the city completely in response to the refusal by British and

US officials to allow Soviet Russia to have more say in future German economic policy and the introduction of the Deutsche Mark to Berlin. The response was the only one possible without military intervention, with the Allies supplying the city by the only means available – air. There were four air corridors into Berlin across the Soviet Zone which had been set up by the November 1945 Quadripartite Agreement, through which the Allies could fly to and from Berlin. These were used for Operation Plainfare or what has become known as the Berlin Airlift. Aircraft of the RAF, USAF and private aeroplanes chartered by the Allied governments supplied 2.3 million tons of essential fuel and supplies to Berlin throughout the blockade which lasted until 12th May 1949. After the blockade was lifted, the city became formally divided into West and East Berlin (with the Berlin Wall eventually being built twelve years later in 1961).

Following this and the increasing tensions that were to lead to the Korean War on the other side of the world, a major expansion programme for the Armed Forces commenced. It was clear that BAFO was no longer a force of occupation, so it reverted in name to the Second Tactical Air Force or 2nd TAF. With this expansion came a major airfield-building programme in the early 1950s, which included the so-called 'Clutch' airfields of Brüggen, Wildenrath, Laarbruch and Geilenkirchen which were to become synonymous with the RAF in Germany.

By 1955 the Allies believed that German participation and commitment was needed to counter the increasing military threat from the Soviet Union and its allies known as the Warsaw Pact. Germany thus joined the North Atlantic Treaty Organisation (NATO) and on 9th January 1956 the new German Air Force came into being.

Following his time at Brüggen, Eric was to become deeply involved with training pilots for this nascent air force.

CHAPTER 15

RETURNING TO THE UK ONCE MORE - PAGE 170

OPERATION FIREDOG AND THE INDONESIAN CONFRONTATION

Whilst the Cold War was to the forefront of most people's minds in the 1950s and 1960s, there were other areas of conflict around the world, particularly related to the winding down of the British Empire. In the Far East, British colonial control over Malaya had long been in difficulty with the resultant outbreak of hostilities in 1948, which became known as the Malayan Emergency. Operation Firedog was the Royal Air Force response to this.

During the Second World War, the British had supplied

Malayan insurgents with arms to resist the Japanese invasion. Post-war, most returned to their homes and pre-war jobs but a breakaway communist-lead group, which came to be known as the Malayan Races Liberation Army (MRLA), formed to instigate a communist take-over. As the conflict progressed, group members became known by the authorities as Communist Terrorists (or 'CTs').

The conflict began when three European officials were murdered by CTs on 16th July 1948, resulting in the immediate declaration of a State of Emergency. Whilst the conflict would primarily be fought on the ground in the jungle by the army, air support was essential. Initially this took the form of photographic reconnaissance, both to find CT encampments and to map the area. Increasingly, as the conflict wore on, the CTs were forced back by the army using air supply drops and offensive air strikes. In 1950, the helicopter appeared, mainly in a casualty evacuation (CASEVAC) role and later to move troops into position, a precursor of things to come. The MRLA's activity reached a peak in 1951 with the ambush and killing of the British High Commissioner to Malaya, Sir Henry Gurney. Under his successor, General Gerald Templer, co-operation between civil and military powers began to undermine the terrorist threat. By 1953 the CTs had been pushed back into northern Malaya and in October, a major offensive was mounted both on the ground and from the air, including the dropping of millions of leaflets in many languages urging the CTs to surrender and offering a Malayan $1000 bounty to those who did.

Malaya became independent on 31st August 1957, which removed the rationale of a war of independence for the CTs. The offensive resulted in much of the country being free of any terrorist activity, with the last serious incident taking place in 1958, following which the remaining CTs fled over the borders to Thailand and China. The Malayan authorities finally declared the emergency over on 31st July 1960. Despite this (and to prevent a resurgence of the insurrection), the authorities maintained a system of jungle outposts (known as 'forts') which were supported by British and Commonwealth (Australian and New Zealand) forces well into the 1960s. Much of Eric's time on 209 Squadron was spent in supply missions to the forts scattered around the Malayan Peninsula.

An indirect result of the Malayan confrontation was what became the Indonesian confrontation. Between 1963 and 1966, British Commonwealth forces fought against Indonesia in a conflict that focused on the future of Brunei and North Borneo. The fighting consisted of small-scale jungle clashes in the border areas and ended in a victory for the Commonwealth. In 1962, northern Borneo consisted of the British protectorate of Brunei and the colonies of Sarawak and North Borneo (later known as Sabah). The rest of the island was made up of the Indonesian provinces of Kalimantan.

President Sukarno of Indonesia resented the British influence and wanted to include the colonies in Kalimantan as part of Indonesia - the most interesting of which was Brunei with its vast oil and gas reserves. The confrontation began on 8th December 1962 when a group of Sukarno-supported rebels moved against Brunei with the intention of capturing the Sultan who immediately appealed to Britain for help. Response to a request for help came in the form of two Gurkha divisions air-lifted from Singapore, followed a couple of days later by other units which swiftly quelled the rebellion and rescued those who had been taken hostage.

The following April, with encouragement again from Sukarno, a number of cross-border incursions by so-called volunteers occurred with the aim of intimidating local people. These were countered by deployment of five battalions of British and Gurkha troops responsible for defending an almost 1,000 mile-long border, much of it cloaked in primary jungle. The British Commander was Major-General Walter Walker who had considerable experience of jungle warfare, having fought the Japanese in Burma and Communists in Malaya. Walker was a great advocate of the use of the helicopter and the nature of the terrain meant that air support (both helicopter and fixed wing) was essential. In addition to supporting the Malayan Forts, this was the type of flying undertaken by (amongst others) 209 Squadron that Eric was to join in April 1965.

In September 1963 Sukarno finally committed regular Indonesian troops and the British forces were supplemented by troops from Malaya, Australia and New Zealand. Skirmishes continued until late 1965, by which time the British-led forces had control of the border. In October that year, the Indonesian army foiled an attempted coup by the Indonesian Communist Party, the main supporters of Sukarno. In March 1966 General Suharto overthrew Sukarno and withdrew all Indonesian forces from the border areas before signing a peace treaty with Malaysia in 1966.

AVIATION CAREER AND UNITS SERVED

The following section details all the major dates and deployments of Eric's aviation career, from his induction into the RAF in 1942, to his last major civilian role in 1984.

Initial RAF Induction and Training in the UK		
Unit	**Location**	**Commenced**
Aircrew Reception Centre	London	29/09/1942
No. 6 Initial Training Wing	Aberystwyth	24/10/1942
No. 9 Flying Training School	Ansty	15/04/1943
Aircrew Dispersal Centre	Manchester	20/05/1943

RAF Training in Canada		
Unit	**Location**	**Commenced**
No. 31 Personnel Depot	Moncton	27/06/1943
No. 32 Elementary Flying Training School	Bowden	24/07/1943
No. 4 Service Flying Training School	Saskatoon	17/09/1943
No. 1 General Reconnaissance School	Summerside	26/02/1944
No. 31 Personnel Depot	Moncton	29/04/1944
No. 5 Operational Training Unit	Boundary Bay	29/07/1944
No. 5 Heavy Conversion Unit	Abbotsford	25/09/1944
No. 1 'Y' Depot	Lachine	06/12/1944

In Transit to the UK		
Unit	**Location**	**Commenced**
No. 9 Personnel Reception Centre	Harrogate	26/12/1944
No. 18 Personnel Despatch Centre	London	16/01/1945

RAF Service in India		
Unit	**Location**	**Commenced**
No. 9 Transit Camp	Karachi	18/02/1945
No. 6 Refresher Flying Unit	Kolar	26/02/1945
231 Group	Calcutta	26/03/1945
159 Squadron	Digri	27/03/1945
232 Squadron	Poona	25/05/1946

In Transit to the UK		
Unit	**Location**	**Commenced**
No. 5 Personnel Despatch Centre	Burtonwood	19/09/1946
No. 21 Aircrew Holding Unit	Chalgrove	21/10/1946
No. 3 General Reconnaissance School	Leuchars	08/11/1946
No. 101 Personnel Despatch Centre	Kirkham	27/04/1947
Demobilised from the RAF: 28/04/1947		

Re-enlistment and later RAF Career		
Unit	**Location**	**Commenced**
No. 8 Refresher Flying School (RAFVR)	Woodley	09/06/1950
Re-joined the RAF	Hendon	12/06/1951
Central Flying School	Moreton-in-Marsh	12/06/1951
Central Flying School (B)	South Cerney	25/07/1951
Central Flying School (A)	Little Rissington	01/10/1951
RAF College	Cranwell	19/11/1951
Central Flying School (B)	South Cerney	20/08/1954

RAF Service in Germany		
Unit	Location	Commenced
2nd Tactical Air Force	Brüggen	14/08/1956
RAF Mission to the German Air Force	Landsberg	07/01/1959

RAF Service in the UK		
Unit	**Location**	**Commenced**
University Air Squadron	Cambridge	04/07/1961
University Air Squadron	Nottingham	01/08/1961
Joint Services Photo Interpretation	Upwood	04/10/1961
Joint Air Reconnaissance Intelligence Centre	Brampton	13/12/1961
Twin Pioneer Conversion Unit	Odiham	01/02/1965

RAF Service in Singapore		
Unit	**Location**	**Commenced**
209 Squadron	Seletar	29/04/1965
Operations Wing Staff	Seletar	01/10/1965

RAF Service in the UK		
Unit	Location	Commenced
No. 1 School of Refresher Flying	Manby	21/03/1968
No. 5 Flying Training School	Oakington	01/07/1968
HQ Strike Command	High Wycombe	19/05/1970
No. 5 Flying Training School Centre	Oakington	01/11/1971
HQ Training Command	Brampton	13/01/1975
HQ Central Flying School	Cranwell	18/10/1976
Central Flying School Exam Wing	Leeming	18/11/1976
Retired from RAF	Leeming	13/02/1978

Civilian Air Career in the UK		
Unit	**Location**	**Commenced**
Civil Aviation Authority Flying Unit	Stansted	01/03/1978
Thurston Aviation	Stansted	15/01/1984

TYPES FLOWN

This section details all the aircraft types that Eric flew during his career, in chronological order.

For further details about some of the terminology and acronyms used in this section, please refer to the *Glossary of Terms*.

In most of the photographs showing aeroplanes when Eric was training, the aeroplanes look black or at least very dark. The aeroplanes were actually painted yellow for conspicuity but the images were taken on orthographic ('ortho') film which was common at the time and which renders yellow very dark.

Note:

During his time with CAAFU and Thurston Aviation, although based at Stansted, Eric often undertook flights from other locations. It's those locations that are given in this section.

ABBREVIATIONS USED IN THIS SECTION

Power

hp = horse power

lb = pounds (of thrust)

Dimensions

ft = feet

in = inches

m = metres

Weight

lb = pounds

kg = kilograms

Speed

kt = knots

Distance

km = kilometres

- **Type:** De Havilland DH82A Tiger Moth
- **Role:** Trainer
- **Crew Complement**: 2
- **Power:** 1 x 130hp DH Gypsy Major piston engine
- **Dimensions:** Wing span 29ft 4in (8.9m), length 23ft 11in (7.3m)
- **Metrics:** Empty weight 1,200lb (544kg), max weight 1,825lb (828kg), max speed 139kt, cruising speed 75kt, range 300 miles (482km), service ceiling 12,000ft (3657m)
- **Flown by Eric:** Initial training No. 9 FTS Ansty 1943, No. 8 Reserve FS Woodley 1950

Image copyright: Alan Markwell.

- **Type:** Fairchild PT26a Cornell
- **Role:** Trainer
- **Crew Complement**: 2
- **Power:** 1 x 200hp Ranger piston engine
- **Dimensions:** Wing span 37ft (11.3m), length 28ft 8in (8.8m)
- **Metrics:** Empty weight 2,022lb (917kg), max weight 2,736lb (1,241kg), max speed 105kt, cruising speed 88kt, range 400 miles (644km), service ceiling 13,000ft (3,962m)
- **Flown by Eric:** Training in Canada,
  No. 32 EFTS Bowden 1943

Image copyright: Commonwealth Air Training Plan Museum.

- **Type:** Cessna Crane
- **Role:** Trainer
- **Crew Complement**: Up to 5
- **Power:** 2 x 245hp Jacobs Radial piston engines
- **Dimensions:** Wing span 41ft 11in (12.8m), length 32ft 9in (10.0m)
- **Metrics:** Empty weight 3,500lb (1,599kg), max weight 5,700lb (2,585kg), max speed 189kt, cruising speed 152kt, range 1,350 miles (2,170km), service ceiling 22,000ft (6,705m)
- **Flown by Eric:** Training in Canada, No. 4 SFTS Saskatoon 1943

Image copyright: Commonwealth Air Training Plan Museum.

- **Type:** AVRO Anson I, II, V, XIX and XXI
- **Role:** Trainer, Communications, Light Bomber
- **Crew Complement**: Up to 5
- **Power:** (Canadian built examples) 2 x 330hp Jacobs radial piston engines, (UK built examples 2 x 420hp Armstrong Siddeley Cheetah radial piston engines)
- **Dimensions:** Wing span 56ft 6in, (17.2m), length 42ft 3in (12.9m)
- **Metrics:** Empty weight 5,880lb (2,667kg), max weight 7,650lb (3,469kg), max speed 160kt, cruising speed 133kt, range 787 miles (1,270km), service ceiling 16,200ft (4,937m)
- **Flown by Eric:** Training in Canada,
  No. 4 SFTS Saskatoon 1943, No. 1 GRS Summerside 1944, No. 3 GRS Leuchars 1946, CFS Cranwell 1954

Image copyright: Commonwealth Air Training Plan Museum.

- **Type:** North American B25 Mitchell
- **Role:** Medium Bomber
- **Crew Complement**: Up to 6
- **Power:** 2 x 1,700hp Wright Cyclone Radial piston engines
- **Dimensions:** Wing span 67ft 6in (20.6m), length 53ft 6in (16.3m)
- **Metrics:** Empty weight 2,022lb (917kg), max weight 2,736lb (1,241kg), max speed 260kt, cruising speed 200kt, range 1,350 miles (2,175km), service ceiling 24,000ft (7,300m)
- **Flown by Eric:** Training in Canada,
  No. 5 OTU Boundary Bay 1944

Pictured: Mitchell HD279 'AQ'. Eric flew his first Mitchell familiarisation flight in this aircraft on 14/8/44.

Image copyright: McKechnie image, DesMazes collection.

- **Type:** Consolidated B24 Liberator VI, VIII and C87
- **Role:** Very Long Range Heavy Bomber
- **Crew Complement**: 7-10
- **Power:** 4 x 1200hp Pratt and Whitney Twin Wasp Radial piston engines
- **Dimensions:** Wing span 110ft (33.5m), length 67ft 2in (20.5m)
- **Metrics:** Empty weight 37,033lb (16,798kg), max weight 65,058lb (29,510kg), max speed 252kt, cruising speed 210kt, range 2,050 miles (3,300km), service ceiling 28,000ft (8,534m)
- **Flown by Eric:** Training in Canada,No. 5 OTU Boundary Bay, 159 Sqn Digri, India 1945, 232 Sqn Poona, India 1946

Pictured (left): B24 Liberator KG929 'AH' flown by Eric twice, on 27th and 29th October 1944.
Image copyright: McKechnie image, DesMazes collection.

- **Type:** AVRO Lancaster
- **Role:** Long Range Heavy Bomber
- **Crew Complement**: Up to 7
- **Power:** 4 x 1,620hp RR Merlin piston engines
- **Dimensions:** Wing span 102ft (31.1m), length 69ft 4in (21.1m)
- **Metrics:** Empty weight 36,900lb (16,738kg), max weight 63,000lb (28,576kg), max speed 245kt, cruising speed 210kt, range 2,685 miles (4,319km), service ceiling 24,500ft (7,467m)
- **Flown by Eric:** Local flying whilst on 159 Sqn

Image copyright: iStock/Getty Images.

- **Type:** North American Harvard IIB and IV
- **Role:** Trainer
- **Crew Complement**: 2
- **Power:** 1 x 600hp Pratt and Whitney Radial piston engine
- **Dimensions:** Wing span 42ft (12.8m), length 28ft 11in (8.8m)
- **Metrics:** Empty weight 3,995lb (91,812kg), max weight 5,235lb (2,375kg), max speed 154kt, cruising speed 120kt, range 710 miles (1,143km), service ceiling 22,000ft (7,610m)
- **Flown by Eric:** CFS Moreton-in-Marsh, South Cerney, Little Rissington, Cranwell 1951 - 1956,
  RAF Mission to the German Air Force Landsberg
  1959 - 1961

Image copyright: Alan Markwell.

- **Type:** Percival Prentice
- **Role:** Trainer
- **Crew Complement**: 2/3
- **Power:** 1 x 250hp Dc Havilland Gypsy Queen piston engine
- **Dimensions:** Wing span 46ft (14.03m), length 31ft 4in (9.5.8m)
- **Metrics:** Empty weight 2,022lb (917kg), max weight 2,736lb (1,241kg), max speed 167kt, cruising speed 11kt, range 396 miles (637km), service ceiling 19,000ft (5,800m)
- **Flown by Eric:** CFS South Cerney 1951, No. 135 Wing Brüggen, Germany 1956

Image copyright: courtesy Oliver Holmes/ABPic.

- **Type:** Gloster Meteor T7
- **Role:** Trainer
- **Crew Complement**: 2
- **Power:** 2 x 3,600lb thrust RR Derwent jet engines
- **Dimensions:** Wing span 37ft 2in (11.3m), length 44ft 7in (13.5m)
- **Metrics:** Empty weight 10,600lb (3,230kg), max weight 15,700lb (7,121kg), max speed 535kt, cruising speed 475kt, range 600 miles (965km), service ceiling 43,000ft (13,100m)
- **Flown by Eric:** CFS Little Rissington 1951, Cranwell 1954, South Cerney 1956, No. 135 Wing Brüggen, Germany 1957 – 1958

Image copyright: iStock/Getty Images.

- **Type:** De Havilland Canada DHC1 Chipmunk
- **Role:** Trainer
- **Crew Complement**: 2
- **Power:** 1 x 145hp DH Gypsy Major piston engine
- **Dimensions:** Wing span 34ft 4in (10.5m), length 24ft 4in (7.7m)
- **Metrics:** Empty weight 1,424lb (646kg), max weight 2,100lb (952kg), max speed 118kt, cruising speed 92kt, range 276 miles (444km), service ceiling 16,000ft (4,877m)
- **Flown by Eric:** CFS Cranwell 1953,
  No. 135 Wing Brüggen, Germany 1957 – 1958,
  Nottingham UAS 1961, Leeming 1978

Image copyright: Alan Markwell.

- **Type:** De Havilland DH100 Vampire T11
- **Role:** Trainer
- **Crew Complement**: 2
- **Power:** 1 x 3,200lb thrust DH Goblin jet engine
- **Dimensions:** Wing span 39ft 11in (11.4m) , length 30ft 8in (9.4m)
- **Metrics:** Empty weight 7,284lb (3,304kg), max weight 12,390lb (5,620kg), max speed 476kt, cruising speed 400kt, range 1,060 miles (1,963km), service ceiling 44,000ft (13,410m)
- **Flown by Eric:** CFS Little Rissington 1953 – 1955, No. 135 Wing Brüggen, Germany 1956 - 1957

Image copyright: Alan Markwell.

- **Type:** Boulton Paul Balliol T2
- **Role:** Trainer
- **Crew Complement**: 2
- **Power:** 1 x 1,245hp RR Merlin piston engine
- **Dimensions:** Wing span 39ft 4in (12.0m), length 35ft 1in (10.7m)
- **Metrics:** Empty weight 6,730lb (3,053kg), max weight 8,410 Lbs (3,805kg), max speed 247kt, cruising speed 198kt, range 660 miles (1,062km), service ceiling 32,500ft (9,900m)
- **Flown by Eric:** CFS Cranwell 1954

Image copyright: Alan Markwell.

- **Type:** Percival Provost
- **Role:** Trainer
- **Crew Complement**: 2
- **Power:** 1 x 550hp Alvis Leonides Radial piston engine
- **Dimensions:** Wing span 35ft (10.67m), length 28ft 6in (8.69m)
- **Metrics:** Empty weight 3,350lb (1,520kg), max weight 4,399lb (1,995kg), max speed 172kt, cruising speed 120kt, range 650 miles (1,046km), service ceiling 13,000ft (3,962m)
- **Flown by Eric:** CFS Cranwell 1954-1955, South Cerney 1956, Manby 1958

Image copyright: Alan Markwell.

- **Type:** Auster VII
- **Role:** Light Transport/Communications/Spotting
- **Crew Complement**: 2/3
- **Power:** 1 x 150hp DII Gypsy Major piston engine
- **Dimensions:** Wing span 36ft (10.9m), length 22ft 5in (6.8m)
- **Metrics:** Empty weight 1,100lb (498kg), max weight 1,850lb (839kg), max speed 112kt, cruising speed 96kt, range 250 miles (402km), service ceiling 16,000ft (4,856m)
- **Flown by Eric:** CFS Cranwell 1954

Image copyright: courtesy Brian Bickers.

- **Type:** Fairey Firefly T7
- **Role:** Trainer version of Naval Fighter
- **Crew Complement**: 2
- **Power:** 1 x 2,455hp RR Griffon piston engine
- **Dimensions:** Wing span 44ft 6in (13.5m), length 38ft (11.5m)
- **Metrics:** Empty weight 11,016lb (4,996kg), max weight 2,736lb (1,241kg), max speed 105kt, cruising speed 88kt, range 860 miles (1,384km), service ceiling 25,500ft (7,772m)
- **Flown by Eric:** RNAS Culdrose 1955

Image copyright: Imperial War Museum.

- **Type:** Hunting Percival Jet Provost T4
- **Role:** Trainer
- **Crew Complement**: 2
- **Power:** 1 x 2,500lb thrust Armstrong Siddeley Viper jet engine
- **Dimensions:** Wing span 35ft 4in (10.7m), length 34ft (10.3m)
- **Metrics:** Empty weight 4,888lb (2,217kg), max weight 9,200lb (4,173kg), max speed 380kt, cruising speed 325kt, range 900 miles (1,450km), service ceiling 36,750ft (11,200m)
- **Flown by Eric:** CFS South Cerney 1955

Image copyright: iStock/Getty Images.

- **Type:** Hawker Hunter F4
- **Role:** Fighter
- **Crew Complement**: 1
- **Power:** 1 x 10,145lb thrust RR Avon jet engine
- **Dimensions:** Wing span 33ft 8in (10.2m), length 45ft 10in (13.98m)
- **Metrics:** Empty weight 14,123lb (6,406kg), max weight 24,600lb (11,158kg), max speed 620kt, cruising speed 550kt, range 445 miles (715km), service ceiling 13,000ft (3,962m)
- **Flown by Eric:** CFS Little Rissington 1956

Note: Aircraft pictured at RAF Brüggen.

Image copyright: Alan Markwell.

- **Type:** English Electric Canberra T4
- **Role:** Medium Bomber
- **Crew Complement**: 2
- **Power:** 2 x 7,400lb RR Avon jet engines
- **Dimensions:** Wing span 64ft (19.5m), length 65ft 6in (19.9m)
- **Metrics:** Empty weight 21,650lb (9,820kg), max weight 55,000lb (24,948kg), max speed 504kt, cruising speed 450kt, range 810 miles (1,310km) service ceiling 48,000ft (15,000m)
- **Flown by Eric:** No. 135 Wing Brüggen, Germany 1957

Image copyright: courtesy Ken Elliott/ABPic.

- **Type:** Vickers Varsity T1
- **Role:** Navigation Trainer
- **Crew Complement**: 2 (plus trainees)
- **Power:** 2 x 1,950hp Bristol Hercules radial piston engines
- **Dimensions:** Wing span 95ft 8in (29.18m), length 67ft 6in (20.6m)
- **Metrics:** Empty weight 27,040lb (12,265kg), max weight 37,500lb (17,000kg), max speed 250kt, cruising speed 207kt, range 2648 miles (4,261km), service ceiling 28,700ft (8,700m)
- **Flown by Eric:** School of Refresher Flying Manby 1964 – 1965, 1968, No. 5 FTS Oakington 1968 - 1974

Image copyright: courtesy Robin A. Walker.

- **Type:** Scottish Aviation Twin Pioneer
- **Role:** STOL Medium Transport
- **Crew Complement**: 2
- **Power:** 2 x 640hp Alvis Leonides radial piston engines
- **Dimensions:** Wing span 76ft 6in (23.32m), length 45ft 3in (13.79m)
- **Metrics:** Empty weight 10,200lb (4,627kg), max weight 14,600lb (6,622kg), max speed 144kt, cruising speed 100kt, range 800 miles (1,287km) service ceiling 20,000ft (6,096m)
- **Flown by Eric:** TP Conversion Unit Odiham, 209 Sqn Singapore 1965 - 1968

Image copyright: Alan Markwell.

- **Type:** Scottish Aviation Single Pioneer
- **Role:** STOL Light Transport
- **Crew Complement**: 1
- **Power:** 1 x 520hp Alvis Leonides radial piston engine
- **Dimensions:** Wing span 49ft 9in (15.7m), length 34ft 4in (10.47m)
- **Metrics:** Empty weight 3,843lb (1,743kg), max weight 5,811lb (2,636kg), max speed 141kt, cruising speed 95kt, range service ceiling 23,000ft (7,010m)
- **Flown by Eric:** 209 Sqn Seletar, Singapore 1965 - 1968

Image copyright: Alan Markwell.

- **Type:** Blackburn Beverley
- **Role:** Heavy Transport
- **Crew Complement**: 6
- **Power:** 4 x 2,850hp Bristol Centaurus radial piston engines
- **Dimensions:** Wing span 162ft (49.37m), length 99ft 5in (30.3m)
- **Metrics:** Empty weight 79,234lb (35,940kg), max weight 143,000lb (64,863kg), max speed 206kt, cruising speed 150kt, range 200 miles (321km) service ceiling 16,000ft (4,875m)
- **Flown by Eric:** 34 Sqn Seletar, Singapore 1967

Image copyright: Alan Markwell.

- **Type:** De Havilland Canada DHC 2 Beaver
- **Role:** STOL Utility
- **Crew Complement**: 1
- **Power:** 1 x 450hp Pratt and Witney Wasp radial piston engine
- **Dimensions:** Wing span 48ft (14.93m), length 30ft 3in (9.22m)
- **Metrics:** Empty weight 2,851lb (1,293kg), max weight 5,099lb (2,313kg), max speed 141kt, cruising speed 110kt, range 733 miles (1179km) service ceiling 18,000ft (5,486m)
- **Flown by Eric:** Army Air Corps Seletar 1967

Image copyright: Alan Markwell.

- **Type:** Beagle 206 Bassett
- **Role:** Utility/Liaison
- **Crew Complement**: 1
- **Power:** 2 x 340hp Continental piston engines
- **Dimensions:** Wing span 45ft 10in (13.96m), length 33ft 8in (10.26m)
- **Metrics:** Empty weight 4,799lb (2,177kg), max weight 7,500lb (3,402kg), max speed 235kt, cruising speed 210kt, range 1,600 miles (2,574km), service ceiling 27,100ft (8,260m)
- **Flown by Eric:** No. 5 FTS Oakington 1969

Image copyright: courtesy Malcolm Clarke/ABPic.

- **Type:** Scottish Aviation Jetstream
- **Role:** Navigation Trainer
- **Crew Complement**: 2
- **Power:** 2 x 320hp Turbomeca Astazou turbo-prop engines
- **Dimensions:** Wing span 52ft (15.85m), length 47ft 1in (14.36m)
- **Metrics:** Empty weight 7,606lb (3,450kg), max weight 14,551lb (6,600kg), max speed 263kt, cruising speed 220kt, range 484 miles (780km), service ceiling 31,600ft (9,632m)
- **Flown by Eric:** No. 5 FTS Oakington 1974,
  CFS Examining Wing Leeming 1976 - 1978

Image copyright: Alan Markwell.

- **Type:** Scottish Aviation Bulldog T1
- **Role:** Trainer
- **Crew Complement**: 2
- **Power:** 1 x 200hp Lycoming piston engine
- **Dimensions:** Wing span 33ft (10.06m), length 23ft 3in (7.09m)
- **Metrics:** Empty weight 1,430lb (649kg), max weight 2,350lb (1,066kg), max speed 130kt, cruising speed 90kt, range 620 miles (998km), service ceiling 16,000ft (4,877m)
- **Flown by Eric:** Scottish Aviation Prestwick 1974

Image copyright: John5199 - Shoreham Airshow 2012 (via Wikimedia).

- **Type:** De Havilland DH 125 Domines
- **Role:** Navigation/Crew Trainer
- **Crew Complement**: 2
- **Power:** 2 x 300lb Bristol Siddeley Viper jet engines
- **Dimensions:** Wing span 47ft (14.33m), length 50ft 9in (15.46m)
- **Metrics:** Empty weight 12,844lb (5,826kg), max weight 25,501lb (11,567kg), max speed 436kt, cruising speed 380kt, range 2,785 miles (4,482km) service ceiling 41,000ft (12,497m)
- **Flown by Eric:** Leeming 1975

Image copyright: Ministry of Defence/Crown copyright.

- **Type:** Beech B55 /58 Baron (58 shown)
- **Role:** Touring, Multi-Engine Trainer/Light Transport
- **Crew Complement**: 1
- **Power:** 2 x 325hp Continental piston engines
- **Dimensions:** Wing span 37ft 10in (11.53m), length 29ft 10in (9.09m)
- **Metrics:** Empty weight 4,017lb (1,822kg), max weight 6,200lb (2,812kg), max speed 261kt, cruising speed 220kt, range 1414 miles (2,276km), service ceiling 25,000ft (7,620m)
- **Flown by Eric:** College of Air Training, Hamble, Multi Engine Refresher Course 1976, 1982-1983

Image Copyright: Courtesy TEXTRON Aviation.

- **Type:** Piper PA39 Twin Commanche
- **Role:** Light Touring, Utility
- **Crew Complement**: 1-2
- **Power:** 2 x 160hp Lycoming piston engines
- **Dimensions:** Wing span 36ft 9in (11.21m), length 25ft 2in (7.67m)
- **Metrics:** Empty weight 2,271lb (1,030kg), max weight 3,600lb (1,633kg), max speed 200kt, cruising speed 120kt, range 1,200 miles (1,932km) service ceiling 25,000ft (7,620m)
- **Flown by Eric:** CAAFU, Cranfield 1978

Image copyright: courtesy Randy J. Africano.

- **Type:** Cessna 150/152
- **Role:** Light Trainer/Utility
- **Crew Complement**: 1-2
- **Power:** 1 x 110hp Lycoming piston engine
- **Dimensions:** Wing span 33ft 6in (10.21m), length 24ft 1in (7.34m)
- **Metrics:** Empty weight 1,105lb (501kg), max weight 1,669lb (757kg), max speed 111kt, cruising speed 90kt, range 415 miles (769km) service ceiling 14,700ft (4,481m)
- **Flown by Eric:** CAAFU, Cranfield 1978

Image copyright: Alan Markwell.

- **Type:** Cessna 172
- **Role:** Light Touring, Training, Utility
- **Crew Complement**: 1
- **Power:** 1 x 160hp Lycoming piston engine
- **Dimensions:** Wing span 36ft (11.0m), length 27ft 2in (8.28m)
- **Metrics:** Empty weight 1,622lb (736kg), max weight 2,454lb (1,113kg), max speed 163kt, cruising speed 90kt, range 791 miles (1,272km), service ceiling 13,000ft (3,962m)
- **Flown by Eric:** CAAFU, Cranfield 1978

Note: The photo shows the actual aircraft in which Eric taught Alan to fly, and in which Alan made his first solo flight, on 5th March 1983.

Image copyright: Alan Markwell.

- **Type:** Cessna 182
- **Role:** Light Touring, Training, Utility
- **Crew Complement**: 1
- **Power:** 1 x 230hp Lycoming or Continental piston engine
- **Dimensions:** Wing span 36ft (11.0m), length 29ft (8.84m)
- **Metrics:** Empty weight 1,968lb (893kg), max weight 3,100lb (1,406kg), max speed 160kt, cruising speed 120kt, range 1,053 miles (1,695km) service ceiling 18,1000ft (5,517m)
- **Flown by Eric:** CAAFU, Cranfield 1978

Image copyright: Adrian Pingstone (via Wikimedia).

- **Type:** De Havilland DH 104 Dove/Devon (the Devon was the military version of the Dove)
- **Role:** Regional Airliner, Light Transport
- **Crew Complement**: 2
- **Power:** 2 x 400hp De Havilland Gypsy Queen piston engines
- **Dimensions:** Wing span 57ft (17.37m), length 39ft 4in (11.99m)
- **Metrics:** Empty weight 6,581lb (2,985kg), max weight 8,951lb (4,060kg), max speed 204kt, cruising speed 180kt, range 1,175 miles (1,891km), service ceiling 21,700ft (6,614m)
- **Flown by Eric:** CAAFU, Cranfield 1979

Image copyright: Alan Markwell.

- **Type:** Piper PA23-250 Aztec
- **Role:** Light Touring, Multi-Engine Training
- **Crew Complement**: 1
- **Power:** 2 x 250hp Lycoming piston engines
- **Dimensions:** Wing span 37ft 4in (11.35m), length 31ft 3in (9.53m)
- **Metrics:** Empty weight 3,006lb (1,363kg), max weight 5,200lb (2,358kg), max speed 216kt, cruising speed 172kt, range 709 miles (1,141km), service ceiling 19,800ft (6,035m)
- **Flown by Eric:** CAAFU, Stansted 1979 – 1980

Image copyright: Thurston Aviation (via Alan Markwell).

- **Type:** PA28 -180 Cherokee series (Warrior details quoted)
- **Role:** Light Touring/Trainer
- **Crew Complement**: 1
- **Power:** 1 x 180hp Lycoming piston engine
- **Dimensions:** Wing span 35ft 5in (10.8m), length 24ft (7.32m)
- **Metrics:** Empty weight 1,684lb (764kg), max weight 2,550lb (1,157kg), max speed 133kt, cruising speed 90kt, range 640 miles (1,185km), service ceiling 11,000ft (3,353m)
- **Flown by Eric:** CAAFU, Stansted 1979 - 1983

Image copyright: Alan Markwell.

- **Type:** PA34 SENECA
- **Role:** Light Touring/Multi-Engine Trainer
- **Crew Complement**: 1
- **Power:** 2 x 220hp Continental piston engines
- **Dimensions:** Wing span 38ft 11in (11.86m), length 28ft 7in (8.72m)
- **Metrics:** Empty weight 3,393lb (1,539kg), max weight 4,751lb (2,155kg), max speed 204kt, cruising speed 175kt, range 804 miles (1,295km) service ceiling 25,000ft (7,620m)
- **Flown by Eric:** CAAFU, Stansted 1979 - 1982

Image copyright: courtesy Adrian Pingstone (via Wikimedia).

- **Type:** PA44 Seminole
- **Role:** Light Touring/Multi-Engine Trainer
- **Crew Complement**: 1
- **Power:** 2 x 180hp Lycoming piston engines
- **Dimensions:** Wing span 38ft 7in (11.77m), length 27ft 7in (8.1m)
- **Metrics:** Empty weight 2,360lb (1,071kg), max weight 3,800lb (1,724kg), max speed 202kt, cruising speed 175kt, range 880 miles (1,630km) service ceiling 49,212ft (15,000m)
- **Flown by Eric:** CAAFU, Stansted 1979 - 1983

Image copyright: courtesy John Coates/ABPic.

- **Type:** Grumman GA-7 Cougar
- **Role:** Light Touring/Multi-Engine Trainer
- **Crew Complement**: 1
- **Power:** 2 x 160hp Lycoming piston engines
- **Dimensions:** Wing span 36ft 10in (11.23m), length 28ft 8in (8.8m)
- **Metrics:** Empty weight 2,569lb (1,165kg), max weight 3,800lb (1,724kg), max speed 169kt, cruising speed 160kt, range 1,350 miles (2,170km), service ceiling 17,400ft (5,300m)
- **Flown by Eric:** CAAFU, Stansted 1979 - 1983

Image copyright: courtesy The Grumman Owners & Pilots Association.

- **Type:** Cessna 310
- **Role:** Light Utility/Business Travel
- **Crew Complement**: 1
- **Power:** 2 x 285hp Continental piston engines
- **Dimensions:** Wing span 36ft 11in (11.25m), length 31ft 11in (9.74m)
- **Metrics:** Empty weight 3,358lb (1,523kg), max weight 3,358lb (1,532kg), max speed 181kt, cruising speed 130kt, range 727 miles (1,170km), service ceiling 19,750ft (6,020m)
- **Flown by Eric:** CAAFU, Perth and Edinburgh 1979 - 1980

Image copyright: courtesy Graham Reeve.

- **Type:** Piper PA31 Navajo
- **Role:** Regional/Corporate Transport
- **Crew Complement**: 1
- **Power:** 2 x 350hp Lycoming piston engines
- **Dimensions:** Wing span 40ft 8in (12.4m), length 34ft 7in (10.55m)
- **Metrics:** Empty weight 4,222lb (1,915kg), max weight 7,000lb (3,175kg), max speed 231kt, cruising speed 180kt, range 950 miles (1,528km), service ceiling 24,000ft (7,315m)
- **Flown by Eric:** CAAFU, Stansted 1979 – 1983

Image copyright: Thurston Aviation via Alan Markwell.

- **Type:** Grumman AA5a/AA5b
- **Role:** Trainer, Light Tourer
- **Crew Complement**: 1
- **Power:** 1 x 160hp Lycoming piston engine
- **Dimensions:** Wing span 31ft 6in (9.60m), length 22ft (6.7m)
- **Metrics:** Empty weight 1,350lb (612kg), max weight 2,200lb (997kg), max speed 136kt, cruising speed 128kt, range 518 miles (833km), service ceiling 12,650ft (3,855m)
- **Flown by Eric:** CAAFU, Stansted 1980

Image copyright: courtesy Brian Bickers.

- **Type:** Fuji 200
- **Role:** Trainer, Light Tourer
- **Crew Complement**: 1
- **Power:** 1 x 160hp Lycoming piston engine
- **Dimensions:** Wing span 30ft 11in (9.42m), length 26ft 2in (7.96m)
- **Metrics:** Empty weight 1,433lb (650kg), max weight 2,535lb (1,066kg), max speed 135kt, cruising speed 90kt, range 756 miles (1,215km), service ceiling 13,700ft (4,176m)
- **Flown by Eric:** CAAFU, Stansted 1980

Image copyright: courtesy John Coleman/ABPic.

- **Type:** Commander 114
- **Role:** Light Touring/Business/Training
- **Crew Complement**: 1
- **Power:** 1 x 260hp Lycoming piston engine
- **Dimensions:** Wing span 35ft 7in (10.85m), length 25ft (7.63m)
- **Metrics:** Empty weight 1,855lb (855kg), max weight 3,140lb (1,424kg), max speed 165kt, cruising speed 120kt, range 842 miles (1,356km), service ceiling 17,400ft (5,304m)
- **Flown by Eric:** CAAFU, Stansted1980

Image copyright: Alan Markwell.

- **Type:** PA38 Tomahawk
- **Role:** Light Trainer
- **Crew Complement**: 1
- **Power:** 1 x 112hp Lycoming piston engine
- **Dimensions:** Wing span 34ft (10.36m), length 23ft 1in (7.04m)
- **Metrics:** Empty weight 1,128lb (512kg), max weight 1,670lb (758kg), max speed 108kt, cruising speed 85kt, range 539 miles (867km), service ceiling 13,000ft (3,962m)
- **Flown by Eric:** CAAFU, Stansted 1980

Image copyright: Alan Markwell.

- **Type:** Beech B76 Duchess
- **Role:** Touring, Trainer
- **Crew Complement**: 1
- **Power:** 2 x 180hp Lycoming piston engines
- **Dimensions:** Wing span 38ft (11.3m), length 29ft (8.84m)
- **Metrics:** Empty weight 2,447lb (1,110kg), max weight 3,902lb (1,770kg), max speed 171kt, cruising speed 150kt, range 1,073 miles (1,726km), service ceiling 19,400ft (5,913m)
- **Flown by Eric:** CAAFU, Stansted 1980

Image copyright: courtesy John Davidson/ABPic.

- **Type:** Lockheed C130
- **Role:** Military Heavy Transport
- **Crew Complement**: 2-3
- **Power:** 4 x 4,500hp Allison T56 turbo-prop engines
- **Dimensions:** Wing span 132ft 7in (40.41m), length 97ft 9in (29.79m)
- **Metrics:** Empty weight 75,562lb (34,274kg), max weight 175,000lb (79,379kg), max speed 351kt, cruising speed 300kt, range 2,161 miles (4,02km), service ceiling 28,000ft (8,534m)
- **Flown by Eric:** CAAFU, Lyneham 1981

Image copyright: iStock/Getty Images.

- **Type:** Cessna 206
- **Role:** Touring, Multi-Role
- **Crew Complement**: 1
- **Power:** 1 x 310hp Lycoming piston engine
- **Dimensions:** Wing span 36ft (11.0m), length 28ft 3in (8.6m)
- **Metrics:** Empty weight 2,254lb (1,022kg), max weight 3,600lb (1,633kg), max speed 171kt, cruising speed 130kt, range 830 miles (1,335km), service ceiling 15,700ft (4,785m)
- **Flown by Eric:** CAAFU, Stansted 1980

Image copyright: Adrian Pingstone (via Wikimedia).

- **Type:** Cessna 401/402
- **Role:** Feederliner, Light Transport, Cargo
- **Crew Complement**: 1/2
- **Power:** x 325hp Continental piston engines
- **Dimensions:** Wing span 44ft 2in (13.45m), length 36ft 5in (11.09m)
- **Metrics:** Empty weight 4069lb (1846kg), max weight 6850lb (3107kg), max speed 235kt, cruising speed 180kt, range 1466 miles (2359km), service ceiling 26,900ft (8199m)
- **Flown by Eric:** CAAFU, Stansted 1982 - 1983

Image copyright: courtesy David Lunn/ABPic.

- **Type:** Beech Be90 King Air
- **Role:** Business Travel, Multi-Purpose
- **Crew Complement**: 1-2
- **Power:** 2 x 680hp Pratt and Whitney Canada turbo-prop engines
- **Dimensions:** Wing span 45ft 11in (14.00m), length 39ft 11in (12.17m)
- **Metrics:** Empty weight 6,797lb (3,083kg), max weight 11,500lb (5,216kg), max speed 248kt, cruising speed 180kt, range 1,543 miles (2,482km), service ceiling 24,850ft (7,574m)
- **Flown by Eric:** CAAFU and Thurston Aviation, Stansted 1983 - 1986

Image copyright: Alan Markwell.

- **Type:** Beech 200 King Air/Super King Air
- **Role:** Business Travel, Multi-Purpose
- **Crew Complement**: 1-2
- **Power:** 2 x 850hp Pratt and Whitney Canada turbo-prop engines
- **Dimensions:** Wing span 54ft 6in (16.61m), length 43ft 10in (13.36m)
- **Metrics:** Empty weight 8,317lb (3,773kg), max weight 12,500lb (5,693kg), max speed 270kt, cruising speed 180kt, range 2334 miles (3,756km), service ceiling 35,000ft (10,668m)
- **Flown by Eric:** CAAFU and Thurston Aviation, Stansted 1984 – 1991

Image copyright: Gordon Elias / Ministry of Defence Open Government Licence.

- **Type:** SOCATA (Morane Saulnier) Rallye
- **Role:** Light Trainer/Tourer
- **Crew Complement**: 1
- **Power:** 1 x 180hp Continental piston engine
- **Dimensions:** Wing span 32ft (9.75m), length 20ft 4in (6.2m)
- **Metrics:** Empty weight 1,096lb (497kg), max weight 1,689lb (770kg), max speed 135kt, cruising speed 90kt, range 678 miles (1,091km), service ceiling 34,440ft 10,500m)
- **Flown by Eric:** CAAFU, Stansted 1983

Image copyright: Adrian Pingstone (via Wikimedia).

- **Type:** Beagle 121 Pup
- **Role:** Light Trainer/Tourer
- **Crew Complement**: 1
- **Power:** 1 x 150hp Lycoming piston engine
- **Dimensions:** Wing span 31ft (9.45m), length 23ft 2in (7.06m)
- **Metrics:** Empty weight 1,090lb (494kg), max weight 1,925lb (873kg), max speed 120kt, cruising speed 90kt, range 440 miles (710km), service ceiling 14,700ft (4,500m)
- **Flown by Eric:** CAAFU, Stansted 1983

Image copyright: courtesy Derek Heley ABPic.

- **Type:** Beech Be99
- **Role:** Commuter, Regional Airliner
- **Crew Complement**: 1 - 2
- **Power:** 2 x 715hp Pratt and Whitney Turbo-prop engines
- **Dimensions:** Wing span 45ft 10in (13.98m), length 44ft 7in (13.58m)
- **Metrics:** Empty weight 6,495lb (2,946kg), max weight 11,300lb (5,126kg), max speed 224kt, cruising speed 180kt, range 1,048 miles (1,687km), service ceiling 25,000ft (7,620m)
- **Flown by Eric:** CAAFU and Thurston Aviation, Stansted 1984-1986

Image copyright: courtesy Andy Davey/ABPic.

- **Type:** Cessna 441 Conquest II
- **Role:** Corporate, Commuter Liner
- **Crew Complement**: 1 - 2
- **Power:** 2 x 636hp Garrett Turbo-prop engines
- **Dimensions:** Wing span 49ft 4in (15.04m), length 39ft (11.89m)
- **Metrics:** Empty weight 5,706lb (2,588kg), max weight 9,850lb (4,468kg), max speed 245kt, cruising speed 180kt, range 2,638 miles (4,245km), service ceiling 35,000ft (10,669m)
- **Flown by Eric:** Thurston Aviation, Stansted 1984

Image copyright: Tomas Del Corso (via Wikimedia).

- **Type:** Cessna C 404 Titan
- **Role:** Corporate, Commuter Liner
- **Crew Complement**: 1 - 2
- **Power:** 2 x 375hp Continental piston engines
- **Dimensions:** Wing span 46ft 4in (14.12m), length 39ft 6in (12.04m)
- **Metrics:** Empty weight 4,833lb (2,192kg), max weight 8,400lb (3,810kg), max speed 241kt, cruising speed 180kt, range 2,119 miles (3,410km), service ceiling 26,000ft (7,925m)
- **Flown by Eric:** Thurston Aviation, Stansted 1985

Image copyright: courtesy Kev Slade/ABPic.

- **Type:** EMB 110 Bandeirante
- **Role:** Regional Airliner, Utility
- **Crew Complement**: 1 - 2
- **Power:** 2 x 750hp Pratt and Whitney turboprop engines
- **Dimensions:** Wing span 50ft 4in (15.33m), length 49ft 6in (15.10m)
- **Metrics:** Empty weight 7,915lb (3,590kg), max weight 12,500lb (5,670kg), max speed 248kt, cruising speed 200kt, range 1,243 miles (2,000km), service ceiling 22,500ft (6,858m)
- **Flown by Eric:** Thurston Aviation, Stansted 1985 - 1987

Image copyright: courtesy Graham Reeve/ABPic.

- **Type:** Hawker Siddeley 125
- **Role:** Corporate Transport
- **Crew Complement**: 2
- **Power:** 2 x 3700lb thrust Garrett turbo-fan engines
- **Dimensions:** Wing span 74ft (14.33m), length 50ft 9in (15.46m)
- **Metrics:** Empty weight 12,844lb (5,826kg), max weight 25,501lb (11,567kg), max speed 436kt, cruising speed 400kt, range 2,785 miles (4,482km), service ceiling 41,000ft (12,497m)
- **Flown by Eric:** Thurston Aviation, Stansted 1985

Note: Picture shows early series aircraft with Bristol Siddeley Viper engines.

Image copyright: Alan Markwell.

- **Type:** Shorts SHD 3-30
- **Role:** Regional Airliner
- **Crew Complement**: 2
- **Power:** 2 x 1200hp Pratt and Whitney turbo-prop engines
- **Dimensions:** Wing span 74ft 8in (22.76m), length 58ft (11.09m)
- **Metrics:** Empty weight 14,727lb (6,680kg), max weight 22,899lb (10,387kg), max speed 190kt, cruising speed 150kt, range 1,053 miles (1,695km), service ceiling 11,500ft (3,505m)
- **Flown by Eric:** Thurston Aviation 1986 - 1987

Image copyright: courtesy Brian Bickers.

- **Type:** Slingsby T67B/T67M Firefly
- **Role:** Trainer
- **Crew Complement**: 1
- **Power:** 1 x 160hp Lycoming piston engine
- **Dimensions:** Wing span 34ft 9in (10.59m), length 24ft (7.32m)
- **Metrics:** Empty weight 1,510lb (685kg), max weight 2,150lb (975kg), max speed 140kt, cruising speed 90kt, range 650 miles (1,046km), service ceiling 12,000ft (3,658m)
- **Flown by Eric:** Thurston Aviation, Cranfield 1987

Image copyright: courtesy Grahame Reeve/ABPic.

- **Type:** DH 114 Sea Heron
- **Role:** Communications, Transport
- **Crew Complement**: 2
- **Power:** 4 x 240hp DH Gypsy Queen piston engines
- **Dimensions:** Wing span 71ft 6in (21.79m), length 48ft 6in (14.78m)
- **Metrics:** Empty weight 8,150lb (3,697kg), max weight 13,499lb (6,123kg), max speed 159kt, cruising speed 135kt, range 915 miles (1,472km), service ceiling 18,500ft (5,639m)
- **Flown by Eric:** Thurston Aviation, Bournemouth, Jersey 1989

Image copyright: courtesy Ralf Manteufel/ABPic.

- **Type:** Partenavia P68B
- **Role:** Light Transport, Aerial Survey
- **Crew Complement**: 1
- **Power:** 2 x 200hp Lycoming piston engines
- **Dimensions:** Wing span 39ft 4in (12.00m), length 31ft 4in (9.55m)
- **Metrics:** Empty weight 2,712lb (1,230kg), max weight 4,387lb (1,990kg), max speed 174kt, cruising speed 130kt, range 1,305 miles (2,100km), service ceiling 19,193ft (5,850m)
- **Flown by Eric:** Thurston Aviation, Stansted 1989

Image copyright: courtesy of John Coates/ABPic.

- **Type:** Aero Commander 695
- **Role:** Corporate Transport
- **Crew Complement**: 1
- **Power:** 2 x 290hp Lycoming piston engines
- **Dimensions:** Wing span 49ft 1in (14.95m), length 36ft 10in (11.22m)
- **Metrics:** Empty weight 4,634lb (2,102kg), max weight 6,750lb (3,062kg), max speed 200kt, cruising speed 150kt, range 1,190 miles (1,915km), service ceiling 19,400ft (5,913m)
- **Flown by Eric:** Thurston Aviation, Stanstead 1990

Image copyright: courtesy of John Coates/ABPic.

ACKNOWLEDGEMENTS

Looking back over correspondence, I can see it's been almost five years since I started in earnest to publish Dad's manuscript.

Compiling this book from Dad's manuscript and logbooks has been a fascinating exercise (taking much more time than I'd expected). During this time, I've made many new contacts, all of whom in their own way have helped me to complete the project as a memorial to Dad and those who served with him.

It's impossible to list everyone but I'd like to thank all those who allowed their photographs to be used – particularly in the 'Types Flown' section. I hope I have given due credit and acknowledgment for the copyright and courtesy of allowing me to use them. I apologise if I have incorrectly attributed an image or missed an image credit.

Whilst it's difficult to single out individuals for fear of missing someone, my particular thanks go to: Michael Des Mazes, official RCAF Historian for Abbotsford and Boundary Bay; Matt Poole, co-author of *RAF Liberators over Burma – Flying with 159 Sqn*; Stephen Hayter Executive Director at the Commonwealth Air Training Plan Museum; Brandon Manitoba; Matt Saunders at TEXTRON Aviation; my editor Claire Sanders (clairesanders.uk); my designer Mark Thomas (Coverness.com) and last, but no means least, my brother Peter for his support.

I could not have done it without everyone's input.

Printed in Great Britain
by Amazon

36260230R00185